**A Father's Mi**

**Strong Fatherhood in Ou**

**by Neil M W**

This edition first published in paperback 2017.

# Table of Contents

## Foreword

**By Tom Gold**

I remember finding my eighteen-month-old son, Jack, perched on a stool in front of the bathroom mirror, clutching my razor and about to give himself a shave. I stopped him just in time!

He'd watched me shaving many times and as a keen observer and quick learner, in the way only our children can be, had assumed that this was what he was supposed to do because it was what I did.

What would he think though if he saw me getting drunk or sleeping late, being violent, shouting at his mother, shedding tears?

It occurred to me shortly afterwards that being his dad was going to involve much more than just being home in time to read him a story or making sure that he didn't watch too much TV. I was going to have to lead by example in pretty much everything I said and did.

I can't think of a better way of encapsulating the enormity of this realisation than as 'a father's mission', the title of the book you now hold in your hands.

In the winter of 2015 I met Neil for lunch in Glasgow. In his characteristic quietly determined style he told me about the new project he was working on; an online resource for dads with traditional male values at its core. It would be in marked contrast to much of the existing content on this subject which, in his opinion, lacked both strength and conviction. The site, which as yet did not have a title, would be up and running soon. I never doubted it for a moment.

This project, as you've probably guessed, became the blog This Dad Does which now boasts thousands of loyal followers from all faiths, backgrounds and nationalities. It continues to inspire, challenge, enrage and confront in equal measure.

Now, in the spring of 2017, I am honoured to be writing a foreword to the first full length book to come out of it.

Despite the huge popularity of This Dad Does, this is not a reissue of its greatest hits. Instead this is all new material. That said, those of you who know the site will find some familiar themes here as well as all the humour honesty and grit you've come to expect.

To those of you who have not come across Neil's work you should prepare for plenty of uncomfortable truth, much of it from his own experience, loads of practical advice and a solid and tireless companion who's making the journey with you.

Your mission, should you choose to accept, starts here...

# Introduction

What is a father's mission in our modern age? As our world becomes more connected, more turbulent and more violent - is the role of the father under threat?

I'm writing these words on the evening of the London Parliament terror attacks. The stability and relative peace that our own fathers enjoyed is coming to an end. We now live in an age of uncertainty: economic, social, political.

In this age of uncertainty, the role of the father is changing. Your role is changing. And while some of these changes are good, not all change is good. Not all change will benefit you or the children you are trying to raise.

Imagine what the role of the father will be in another ten or twenty years. Will it continue to be a positive influence on children? Or are you at the threshold of being culturally side lined.

**You Matter Now More than Ever**

This book is about you. You might not know it but when I was writing and putting it together I imagined that I was writing it especially for you. We don't know each other very well but by the time you're finished this short book, we will.

This book is about you and your journey to be a better father. I hope it's a journey we're on together. And if it's not a journey we're on together, it's my wish that we soon will be. If you cruise the pages of this book, you'll see a big focus on you. Y-O-U. That's not a mistake. This isn't a parenting book. This is a book on fatherhood and the elements that make up a successful, driven, committed, loving and protecting Dad. All of those traits come from you.

This is what I truly believe: to become a better father you must become a better man. That's not a criticism - we all have different starting points. What is important is the journey you're taking to become a better man. And therefore, a better father.

What is your motivation to become a better Dad? My motivation is simple: Dads matter more in our modern times than ever. We live in a time when pornography, junk food and wall to wall entertainment is on tap. Our kids will grow up with near permanent connection to the World Wide Web. And while that's positive in some ways, in others it can be a negative influence. It's our responsibility to raise our kids right and to pass on our values onto them.

Why? Because it will probably save their lives. Recent studies have shown that kids who have an involved Dad at home are less likely to:

- Commit suicide
- Drop out of school
- Get pregnant before eighteen
- End up in prison or juvenile detention

Here's the thing: there are no quick fixes to personal improvement. There's no sachet of 'Instant Better Dad - just add hot water'. It's a slow, hard grind. It takes work - more work than you'd have ever imagined. But if you're up for the challenge then this is the right book for you.

'Why bother?' I hear the less committed ask. Turn on your TV and you're bombarded with images of deadbeat or 'Star Wars Dads' who'd rather sit and play computer games or watch live streaming Sci-Fi repeats than put the work in to improve their lives and the lives of those around them.

This book is the antidote to that style of fatherhood.

I must admit that this book has transformed from a short 'best of' my blog - ThisDadDoes.com - into something deeper and stronger than I'd ever imagined. It's been a crystallisation of my understanding of what our generation of fathers need now more than ever. Is the book's subject matter diverse? You bet. I'll happily jump from spirituality to easy-to-cook recipes. But there's a method to this madness - to be a good Dad you must be skilled and competent in a range of disciplines and skills.

**Six Pillars for Strong Fatherhood in Our Modern Times**

I've divided this book into six parts or 'pillars'. These six pillars form the foundations of strong fatherhood. But they also complement each other. In the same way that a series of pillars keep a roof or a ceiling up, these pillars form six areas of your life that are critical to becoming a strong father.

These pillars are:

1. A Father's Mission
2. Mental Strength
3. Spirituality and Self Control
4. The Knowledge
5. The Outdoors
6. Fitness and Physical Health

All of these disciplines have individual value but when put together they begin to shape you into the father you want to be.

Some of these will challenge you, but at the same time I hope you are comforted. What do I mean by that? I want you to see that you're already doing a good job as a Dad and that it might only take a few small adjustments to bring your life back into focus.

**How to Use this Book**

You'll get the best experience from this book if you start at the beginning and read it all the way through once. You'll find practical advice and ideas on nearly every page. But I'd also encourage you to take time to read a second time and focus on the chapters that you feel you need most work and attention. If something inspires you, highlight it and save it for later.

At the end of most chapters you'll find an 'Action' for you to do. Knowledge without application is worthless, but we'll get to that. I wrote this book so that you would enjoy reading it. Find a quiet place where you won't be distracted, turn your phone off and focus.

Breathe.

Now let's begin.

# Pillar 1: A Father's Mission

I remember the first time I felt the true weight of being a Dad. I'd strapped my son into his car seat for the first time and gingerly closed the door. He was sleeping and I didn't want him to wake. I had to make the short trip across town with him and his mother. I've never driven so carefully in my life. I had something of unimaginable value in the car – a new human life. It was at that point I realised that I wasn't just the co-creator of this new being. I was also the protector, teacher and guide. My actions would determine if he lived or died. And whether he survived, or thrived.

When members of military units go on a mission they have an end goal in mind. They have a vision of what they want to achieve: what will constitute mission success or failure. A military mission takes precision planning, training, rehearsing and the best personnel and equipment. As a reservist in an elite infantry unit, I learned the importance of good mission preparation. Even then, success is not always guaranteed.

Fatherhood is a mission. It's something you've been tasked with (whether you chose it or not). It's a quest you must accomplish, a test you must pass. And if you're like me, you're spending a good proportion of your time figuring out how to be a better father.

It's time for you to see fatherhood as a mission. It is your greatest challenge. You will always be a Dad so it's time to start taking it seriously. There are too many Dads out there who half-ass their way through fatherhood. They like the idea of being a switched on, strong father. But when it comes down to it, they'd rather be with their own friends or playing video games to take fatherhood seriously or teach their children any life skills.

That was one of the drivers for me and what led me to start my blog ThisDadDoes.com. I knew there were Dads out there who thought like me and valued the things I valued. But they were difficult to find at times. Now I'm blessed to be connected with a great many incredible and admirable fathers who are totally committed to their mission.

**The Father's Mission – What it Means to You**

It is now up to you to take ultimate responsibility for what you have created. Like the writer of a great novel, this legacy is yours to guard, propagate and love. You cannot be passive in the experience any more than an artist can produce his greatest work and forget instantly what he has done.

Starting right now, understand that your life's purpose had changed irrevocably. You have a new assignment. A new mission. Soon after my son was born (and after the shock had worn off a little bit) I saw my mission more clearly. Let me share it with you now:

**You Have Become the Life Giver**

As a young man, my father found himself alone. His parents' untimely deaths left him an only child. His only option was to face the world unaccompanied. He was the last of his bloodline. Like Chingachgook in Fenimore-Cooper's *Last of the Mohicans*, he was left with the heaviest of responsibilities - to keep the family name alive.

In meeting and marrying my mother, he gave his clan the chance and new life it needed. Now, we fill two cars and continue to grow. Like a pebble dropped in a lake, his impact on the universe continues to ripple outwards.

Your impact as a father is no different. How you got here may not be as dramatic. But your potential to cause a similar impact is equal. You are a giver of life, new life. From that new life there comes near endless possibilities and outcomes. In this way, fatherhood is a bit like those 'Choose Your Own Adventure' novels you enjoyed as a boy where a turn of the page could lead you down a completely different path.

What other beings do we know of that give life? Gods. Many religions (Christianity included) teach that we bear the likeness of our Creator. And so it is with your sons and daughters – your physical likeness is indelibly marked on them for all time. As is your paternal influence. In those 14 to 16 years where you have near complete control, your children will learn more from you than in the remainder of their lives. You, like a god, have created life. What will you do with that unimaginable power?

**We are the Guardians of the Future**

Entrusted to us are our sons and daughters. Even the petrified 20-something fumbling with the car seat has the ultimate responsibility. I recently wrote that having a son is like being given a loaded rifle – I wasn't kidding either. To have the power to influence another human being is a dangerous task. How will you approach this responsibility?

The decisions that you make as a father has a knock-on effect on the future of your family, town and nation. Individually we have little influence but when magnified through the lens of successive generations from ours to the next, that influence increases exponentially. You have the responsibility to raise caring, compassionate, strong, loving, hardworking and valuable sons, daughters, husbands and wives.

Take the example of my own father – the Last of the Mohicans. His influence has shaped the lives of countless people. Multiply that through several generations and seismic shifts can be felt.

What will you do with that responsibility? Will you take it as the greatest honour – to be entrusted with raising the future generation. Or will you goof off, play computer games and watch science fiction movies while your kids eat junk food and watch videos on their iPads?

**Where do We Go From Here?**

In reading this book you've already taken a valuable step. You've raised your hand and volunteered to be the best. You've given up the easy life to one which is much tough, but more rewarding too. You've committed to being the best father you can be, not just for your kids but for yourself too.

Being the best is difficult. Other Dads will resent you and 'hate on' you because you hold up a magnifying glass to their unwillingness to improve. If you encounter resistance on your mission (which you will) shake it off and keep going. You alone have the responsibility of a successful mission. When it comes down to it, your mission is one of survival and self-perpetuation. Dads like us are an endangered species. That's why it's mission critical that you succeed. We must continue to raise our sons to be strong, formidable but compassionate men and our daughters as equally strong, intelligent, brave, feminine women.

This pillar will shape and influence how you read the rest of the book. Don't agree with what you read over the next few pages? That's fine, you're free to keep reading. But don't expect much of it to make sense. Without understanding that you're on a mission, you'll struggle to make sense of what the point of this book is.

I'm going to lay it all out here in this, the first of the six pillars. We'll look at what your mission will entail. We'll finish with a concept I've worked on called the Feminisation of Fatherhood. When I wrote about that subject on my blog, the article quickly went viral. Why? You'll need to read it to find out.

## *Chapter 1: The Father's Vision*

How important is a father's vision? It's difficult to write about the father's mission without examining his vision. Whenever you do anything you have a vision of what the outcome will be. When I cross the street, I have a vision of crossing the other side safely. When I start a new job, I have a vision of what that job will be like, how I will enjoy it and what I will learn from the experience.

When I started my blog ThisDadDoes.com, I had a vision. It wasn't a clear one but I knew that I had stories inside my being that needed sharing with other Dads. I'd often thought about writing an autobiography – but for who? For me? Better to write something that will help you, the reader than a load of exaggerated nonsense about someone you care little about.

Vision narrows your focus. When I was going through selection for the UK airborne forces, I visualised the outcome of my training – battered and bruised but being presented with the honour of being an airborne soldier. It became a reality.

Before I was a father I had a vision of what it would be like. Tough, challenging, emotional but ultimately rewarding. It's been all I wanted and more. In deciding to write this book I had a vision – that you might read it, enjoy it and be able to use my experiences to improve yourself and your ability as a father. And that you would become clear in your own mission.

When you think of a vision, what do you see? Growing up the son of a pastor, a vision meant something along the lines of the prophet Ezekiel's sci-fi encounter with multi eyed men in spinning spaceships in the Bible. Or the temptations of Christ. But in this context, a vision is when you have an idea or a picture in your head of how you want something to turn out.

Here's what I mean by a father's vision:

*You have an idea in your mind of the kind of children you want to raise. You make it your mission to bring them in that way, no matter the personal cost to yourself.*

I have a vision of how I want my children's lives to be and what I want to teach them. I had a vision of raising them somewhere rural where we lived close to my mum and dad. In my vision, this would be somewhere I could teach them to shoot, hunt and fish. Where the wilds of the Scottish Cairngorm mountains were mere touching distance. Where we had a garden that would provide sustenance and interest for all of us.

So, in late 2016, I moved everything to make that vision a reality: job, house - the lot. Will it ever be perfect? No. Was it a giant leap closer to my vision? Yes, yes and yes.

There is a selfish element to this but in making such sacrifice of friends, familiar places and good restaurants, I've achieved more than I could have otherwise. Why do your ambitions need to be limited to your own sense of self-fulfilment? Isn't it nobler and more satisfying to live for the benefit of others as well as yourself?

In the 1998 film Gladiator, the hoary old master gladiator Proximo says this to the hero Maximus:

*"Ultimately, we're all dead men. Sadly, we cannot choose how but, what we can decide is how we meet that end, in order that we are remembered, as men...We mortals are but shadows and dust. Shadows and dust, Maximus!"*

If that's all we are at the end of our time on this spinning globe of rock – shadows and dust - is it not better to leave it a little bit better than when we arrived. I'm writing these words in a house I just bought. But it's not really mine. One of two things will happen: I will sell it to someone else or I will die in it. Either way I'm only really borrowing it. It's in my interests to look after it because when I'm gone, someone else will need to do the same. The bricks of the walls and the soil of the garden will remain long after I've been laid six feet under with my toes pointing east.

The same is true for your kids. While you might refer to them as **your** kids, they aren't really. You had very little in their coming into existence. And you've only got them on loan for a few years until they are fully fledged adults, able to make their own decisions and mistakes.

In the same way that you are the steward or custodian of your little corner of Planet Earth, (I have my little plot of bricks and dirt in rural Scotland), you're also the steward of your kids. They will be under your care for a given period of time and then, one day, they won't be. You cannot control it any more than you can control your own destiny. You had no control over your birth or your death. What makes you think you can control the same for those your love?

The father's mission and vision go hand in hand. My vision dictates my mission. I have a clear picture of the kind of people I want my kids to grow into. And the type of people I don't. How can 'hands off' fatherhood ever work – I you don't raise your kids, someone else will. Who would you leave it to? MTV? Kim and Kloe? Their school teachers?

Or do you exercise your right to shape their destiny. Why shy away from what is probably your biggest responsibility? Are you a coward or are you prepared to say this:

*"I believe that adults should behave in a certain way and have certain skills for life. So, I'm going to spend my kids' childhood shaping and teaching them into the people I believe they should be."*

To many, that would sound draconian and unfashionable. But to you (and me) it's like sweet, sweet music to your ears. Why? Because that's exactly what you want and believe in. It's how you were raised yourself and how you want your kids to raise their kids. Like a runner in a relay, you are merely passing the baton on to your children so that they can pass it on to theirs and so on until the end of time. Your mission as a father is a great and noble undertaking. So grasp it and propagate the vision that will one day manifest into reality.

What does that vision look like? I'm not going to tell you how your kids should be raised of what your vision should be. I can only tell you what my values and practices are. If they align, then great. But I encourage you to develop your own father's vision. Over the course of this book, you'll come to understand my values and beliefs. Will they match with yours? Maybe. Maybe not.

Instead, take your own path. Think about your values, beliefs, skills and strengths. What do you want to teach your sons and daughters. What skills and knowledge will propel them into adult life?

The list might be long but your time is short. By the time your son or daughter is six years old, you will have used up one third of the time you'll have with them before they reach adulthood. It will take personal sacrifice to teach them the skills you want. But isn't that a price worth paying? You forgo personal wealth and gratification for a time while you shape the next generation of the human race. That sounds to me like **time well spent**.

I don't write much about what we now call 'parenting'. Mainly because I don't believe there is one way to do anything. Your approach to raising your kids is different to mine and is based on your values. But always have a vision. Always have an understanding of where you are going.

No Dad lying on his deathbed says "I wish I could have watched more House of Cards reruns." But he will regret not taking his responsibility as a father seriously. He will regret time wasted and opportunities not taken. Every refusal for your attention you give is like a snowflake in your hand – melted into nothing in an instant. You'll never have that opportunity again. Remember this the next time you hear yourself say 'Not now. I'm too busy'.

Now I challenge you to develop a vision of your fatherhood. Refuse to see your kids as an inconvenience or a life accessory. They are on loan to you and the decisions you make as their teacher and friend will affect their lives and shape the future of the human race. No pressure.

**Action:** Close this book right now and think about your vision for fatherhood and your kids. What do you want them to achieve? Are you doing everything you can to help them get there?

## *Chapter 2: What Do You Want for Your Son?*

If you're going to develop a vision of your role as a Dad, it helps to be able to focus on an outcome. But what should that look like? I've got a son and a daughter and I want different things for them. If you have a son, keep reading. Otherwise you might want to skip on to the next chapter where we'll examine a father's vision for his daughter(s).

Let me ask you this: What do you want for your son? No matter what age he is, you must wonder what he'll do or be when he's older. You want the best for him. But what does that even look like? Financial security? Education? Stable relationships? It's impossible to determine the future but that doesn't stop you worrying does it? All these unanswered questions and only the inexorable march of time will give you the answers you want like:

What will bore him?
What will interest him?
What will you constantly disagree over?
And the most loaded of all: What will he be when he grows up……?

There's a trap here though so be warned. It's easy to overstep the mark of 'involved' Dad into 'pushy'. Here's what I mean:

### Pushy Dads – Are they Committed or Mentally Unfulfilled?

The phrase 'pushy parents' is all too familiar. Maybe you know a set of parents who are pushy. Maybe you are a pushy Dad yourself... Is it a bad thing to be pushy?

Imagine this scene which could be from a movie (it's not):

The year is 1920. The father of a young London man wants his son to study medicine and become a doctor. The son couldn't think of anything he'd rather NOT do. But rather than confront his father, he followed his next option. He ran away to Northern Canada.

Living in a wagon in the wilds for several months, he eventually returned home to tell his father he didn't want to be a physician. Instead he began to study what he'd always wanted: optometry.
Who was the young man in this story? Answer: my grandfather.

I recently read an interview with the father of British Olympic cyclist Chris Hoy. He spoke of the sacrifices he made to allow his son to be a success. That included driving all weekend and sleeping in the back of a van so Hoy could attend competitions and meets while still at school. His father spoke fondly of those times but it couldn't have been easy for either of them. Was it worth it? They seem to think so. But is that what you want for your son?

A recent news report announced that assaults on football referees were up. But this wasn't at top flight professional games. This was at pee-wee leagues! Irate fathers physically attack other men because they disagree with their refereeing decisions. Maybe they're angry at the impact these decisions could have on their son's' future careers as the next Wayne Rooney. The sad but inevitable truth is that the junior football field is a place of dashed dreams. Few boys are good enough to become professional and even fewer to play at an elite level. Is all that time, effort, angst (and even a criminal record) worth it for the pushy Dad?

There is clearly a fine line between a commitment to your son's future and personal and emotional instability. Think back to the cautionary tale from my own family's history - Did my great-grandfather want what was best for his son? Probably. Did he express it in the best way? Probably not. Through his desire to get the most out of his son's life he ended up pushing him away. Thankfully my grandfather came back and seems to have made amends but it must have been a difficult time for both.

The longer I go on in fatherhood the more I think that we're all a bit pushy. When teaching my son to ride his bike, I had to stop myself after hearing this one too many times:

"STOP, YOU'RE DOING IT ALL WRONG. THIS IS WASTE OF TIME FOR BOTH OF US IF YOU KEEP MESSING AROUND."

In case you didn't know, this is not the best motivational chat for a three-year-old. Which brings me to this difficult question: Where does your pushiness come from? Does it come from a sense that you didn't quite make it in life? That somehow your younger years were lacking? That you failed when you should have succeeded? Dads who punch football referees or push their sons into careers they do not want could well be projecting their own sense of failure onto their boys.

Hoy's father was committed to his son's success. It paid off. He views the sacrifices he made as being worth it. The other end of the spectrum is the football Dad. Jaded at his own failings, his lack of fulfilment in life is like a big putrid albatross around his boy's neck. The boy might be able to shake it off when he's older. Or he might not in which case he goes through life feeling like a failure because he didn't live up to his Dad's high expectations.

**Life Can be Approached like a Tightrope or a Field of Dreams**

'Where do you see yourself in 5 years?'

Have you ever been asked that in a job interview? I always manage to bluff it somehow with something about not caring as long as I'm bringing value/adding value/creating value. The true answer is this: How the heck should I know? I barely know where I'll be in six months. Sometimes I'm even wrong on that!

The reason behind this is that I don't see life as a tightrope that you have to walk, constantly afraid you'll overbalance and fall off. This linear approach to life was captured in some of Carol Dweck's work on mindset in the 1970's and 80's when she discovered that people who had a 'fixed' (think tightrope) mindset towards life were more likely to give up and feel like failures than those with a 'growth' (field of dreams) approach to life.

How do you see your father's vision? Hopefully you've had time to think about it and what it will look like in the future. I see life as a field of near endless possibilities where I can do and achieve anything I want – if I'm prepared to put the work in. - I like to call it the **Field of Dreams.**

That field has limits. For example – I'll never be a male model, professional fighter or great pianist. There are also places I'd never want to go – like drug or alcohol addiction and mental breakdown. But otherwise I've got a free run to do the things I want to do.

For example, you could:

- Compete internationally in sports
- Learn martial arts and survival skills
- Live on the Uganda/Congo border for a year
- Travel by Jeep through Northern Pakistan to China
- Jump out of a plane in the dark at 800 feet with a nylon sheet on your back

(I've done all these things)

Where did I get this sense of the world truly being my oyster? From my father, of course. I have a Dad who has supported me through every decision I've made – good or bad. I knew from a very young age that I could do what I wanted with my life and he'd be proud. The great thing about the Field of Dreams? There are still things that I can and will achieve in life. In fact, I'm only just getting started.

Doing things like driving the Trans-African highway with a stick in my trunk to fight off baboons has been great. But I'm always looking for a new challenge and a new experience. That Field has been one of **realised** dreams and dreams still to come.

Do you see your life like my Field of Dreams or the tightrope? If it's the latter, how is the balancing coming on? Are you managing OK or are you stuck in a funnel of continuity bias where you believe that you must continue doing the thing you're doing because it's the thing you've always done?

### What do I Want for my Son?

Maybe it's easier to start with what I don't want:

I don't want him to grow up thinking that he has to follow a certain path in life.

I don't want him to go to University 'just because that's what everyone else is doing'.

I mustn't project my failures and anxieties onto him. Instead I'll leave him to make his own mistakes and experience a bit of life's rough and tumble.

I do want him to know that whatever he does and whatever path he chooses, I will be there for him to help and support him if he needs it. Or leave him alone if he needs that too.

I also want him to have financial freedom so that money will never be something he worries about. But he should also be raised understanding the value of money and how to use it wisely and for good.

That's my job as a Dad to teach him these things.

I also want him to experience the Field of Dreams – that he would see his life as an open expanse of possibilities that he can grasp. Or not. That's up to him.

### Project your Positive Life Experiences on to Your Son

What if you were able to project the positive things about your life onto your son. That would be better than projecting your insecurities, wouldn't it? Living a life with few regrets is a great place to start. What do you regret? Anything?

When I look back at my life till now. I don't have many regrets. When opportunities arise, you grab them with both hands and see it through. Here's an example from my own life. A while ago, I wrote down in my notebook 'Start website/blog for Dads'. Now I'm sitting here writing a book which has come out of that idea.

When you live with no regrets, you don't have insecurities and inadequacies to pass on to your son. If you subscribe to the Field of Dreams idea, your mindset is one of abundance and possibilities. That's what you project onto him.

How do you dispel negative memories and regrets? I learned this trick from mindset guru Mike Cernovich. Whenever you find yourself thinking negative thoughts about your past say this to yourself:

"The past does not exist."

Wait? That's it? - Think about it. It's true - the past **doesn't** exist. It's not a place you can go back to or a thing that you can touch or see. Your memory of the past is probably wrong (studies have shown that we are actually pretty poor at remembering past events accurately). Why are you beating yourself up about something that happened a long, long time ago and that you can't change. If the past doesn't exist, it can't hurt you. It can't make you feel inadequate or insecure and you won't have insecurities to project onto your son.

This mantra or slogan is actually a form of self-hypnosis. The very act of saying 'the past does not exist' makes it a reality in your mind. The more you say it (try saying it out loud!) the more you'll believe it to be true.

Are you ready to answer my question: What do you want for your son? Here's what I want: For him to do and achieve all that will make him happy, contented and complete.

**Action**: Take some time to think about what you want for your son. Write down five things you want for his life.

## *Chapter 3: What Do You Want for Your Daughter*

If I'm going to speak about sons, it's only right that I do the same for daughters. After all, if you have kids you've got a 50% chance of having one (actually it's a little higher but I digress). Much of what you've read in chapter 2 applies to daughters too.

(If you skipped chapter 2 because you don't have a son, what were you thinking? Did you seriously believe that I want you to miss out parts of this book? Go back and read it now!)

But there are differences. I'm opposed to the idea that boys and girls can have a bizarre genderless upbringing where you dress them both the same and buy the boys dolls and the girls monster trucks 'because equality'. I'll be interested to speak to the kids in these families in 15 years' time to see how much they valued having their gender norms messed around with like some kind of familial social experiment. Well-meaning parents who brought their kids up as 'gender neutral' will have to deal with the consequences of their choices - as will we.

So, you've probably figured out that I've got traditional views on femininity. Let me lay it out for you before we go any further. If you disagree, then great. I'm glad that we're not all the same or think the same thing. Here goes: I believe that a feminine upbringing is the ultimate fulfilment for women and girls.

In modern western culture, femininity is under attack. It's now seen as being gauche or 'basic' to be a girly-girl. Women and girls who dress and behave in a feminine way can expect to be ridiculed by their peers. If they take care of their bodies by eating healthily and doing exercise, there's a target on their backs.

How many women now suffer in silence in the current cultural climate - where their desire to express their femininity meets a wall of resistance and ridicule. Even in movies and on TV, feminine girls are seen as 'bimbos' where as booky, genderless girls are the true heroines.

It's difficult to reverse a trend on your own. You can't affect a whole culture. But you can change it one person at a time. How? We'll get to that, but first a personal story.

**Girls Change Everything**

I remember my daughter being born. I wasn't well at the time and some of the other events at the time are a blur, but her birth is crystal clear. She wasn't breathing at first and she was blue. The now panicky midwife starts to slap her back hard. SLAP! SLAP! SLAP!

Everything starts to go in slow motion. I see the midwife pull the orange alarm chord and the delivery room instantly fills with people. They grab my daughter, who is still blue and unresponsive, and place her on a platform about 10 feet away from the bed. 'I can see it moving,' I say to my wife as I look over. I'm lying of course. The baby is still blue and lifeless. 'It's going to be fine,' I say again, more to reassure myself than anything. A doctor places an oxygen mask over the baby's face. It looks big enough to envelope the entire head.

No sooner have the words of false reassurance left my mouth that I see a little arm swing in a wide arc. The baby coughs and starts to cry. 'It's a girl!' One of the medical staff shouts over her shoulder, 'And she's got blonde hair!'

Talk about drama! I can smile about it now but you can imagine it was pretty tense at the time. What I didn't realise when that blue bundle plopped into the midwife's waiting hands was this: Girls Change Everything. What do I mean by this? Here's how it all happened. First there was my mum. She bore me and raised me. And there was my older sister. And then came my wife - all female and all easy to relate to. But a daughter?

What do you do with a daughter? Do you treat her the same as your son? How do you relate to her? And what do you want for her for her future.

**What do You Want For Your Daughter?**

As with sons, it's important not to project your failures onto her and try to somehow make amends for your life mistakes. Just because you wanted to join the army when you left school doesn't mean she has to.

Regret that you never took school athletics seriously even though you were the fastest over 1500m in your year? Don't make that your motivation for signing her up to your local running club. It may sound like I'm repeating myself from the previous chapter. And I am.

News just in: Boys and girls are different. The idea that 'gender is a social construct' is pure and utter fallacy for a variety of physiological and psychological reasons that I'm not going to go into (some of them are fairly obvious!). And so even though there are somethings you may want for your son, it's completely OK to want something totally different for your daughter. And you'll always relate to her differently than you do to your son.

For example, she'll always be your little girl. You will always want to protect her to a greater or lesser extent. But you also hope that, one day, you won't need to. On that day, you'll hand her over to the next strong man in her life: Her new protector and friend.

I'm hopeful my daughter will have someone strong in her life in the future who can replace me. He'll be someone I get on well with – although I probably won't like him at first. I'm a bit funny like that. Maybe we'll share an interest. Or maybe he'll pretend to just so I'll like him a bit more.

If you want your daughter to value femininity, guess what? You need to value and respect it too. What does that look like? Let me put it like this. When was the last time you complimented her mother on her appearance in front of her? Do you encourage her to look after herself and to have feminine characteristics? If you don't openly demonstrate how much you value femininity, how will your daughter come to value it in the same way you do?

Of course, you want your daughter to be fulfilled in whatever she does – whether she's working, studying, playing sports or raising children - that goes without saying. But it's your job to teacher her the perseverance and skills she needs to be strong when she needs to be.

**Daughters aren't Sons**

Duh – right? The biggest pitfall for an involved, committed Dad like you is the temptation to treat her as a pseudo-son. You want her to grow up tough, mentally strong and resilient. But not at the cost of her femininity. It's a mistake to see raising your kids as turning them into 'mini-mes'. They have their own powerful wills and identities. Instead, cultivate the Field of Dreams mentality in her. Let her know there are near limitless possibilities for what she can do and achieve in this world but it's up to her to make them happen for herself.

The best way for her to learn this? By your example. When you live your own life in a positive way, the people closest to you pick up on it and will imitate you. That's why we need to lead our daughters by example: as strong, confident, positive men. So that one day, they grow into strong, feminine, confident and positive women.

What was this chapter really about? Was it about raising girls, the end of femininity or just a chance to tell my cool but dramatic birthing story? Probably a combination of all three. If I had to sum it up I'd say this:

You are the protector of your daughter. But one day you won't be. Make sure she knows how to look after herself.

**Action**: Take time to think about what you want for your daughter. Write down five things you want for her.

## *Chapter 4: The Feminisation of Fatherhood*

Before we get into this chapter, I need to set it in a little bit of context. This chapter is based on an article on my blog. It was a piece that I wrote in less than an hour and published almost completely unedited. When I went back and read it later, it seemed clunky, forced and a bit disjointed.

But that didn't stop it from going viral and being my most shared post *ever* within a few hours. Part of the reason was the image I used - a screengrab from an Instagram picture I'd seen earlier that day. It was meant to be a comical photo of Dads pretending to be pregnant. To be honest, the picture itself is quite funny. But the message behind the imagery? That's a different story.

Maybe you don't think fatherhood is under threat. Maybe you don't think that traditional family (and fatherly) values are under attack. And maybe you don't think there is a concerted effort to undermine the role of men (and Dads in particular) in society. If so, I've got good news for you. I'm going to take you on a magical mystery tour into a world that - according to you - doesn't exist. Which is why I want you to imagine.

Imagine if you were going to conspire to undermine the role of the father. How would you do it? Would you go on an all-out frontal attack writing essays, books and protesting on the streets against fathers and how they are the source of all modern evil? Would you stand on soapboxes and street corners and decry traditional family upbringings, clearly defined gender roles? Would you actively discriminate against Dads, abuse them and treat them like crap until they got the message?

Or would you do it by stealth so that people everywhere, men in particular, didn't see it coming until it was too late. You could start to poke fun at fathers. Gently at first but as time went on you would be more and more savage. You could portray them in the media and in children's programming as hapless buffoons (Daddy Pig in *Peppa Pig*, Homer Simpson) before escalating to savagery and all-out attack on what you would call 'Deadbeat Dads'. You could even write a list of the '1000 funniest Bad Dad Quotes' and put it up on Pinterest to totally share with all your friends (lolz). That's just a suggestion.

Which of these approaches would be the most effective in making sure that fathers were seen as being surplus to requirements – even a negative influence on children growing up? Or would you try a different like of attack? A third way?

**The Third Way: From Victory to Victimhood**

It's June 1944. My father is nearly 8 years old and the Second World War is fast approaching its climax. Men, some of them teenagers are climbing into boats, planes and gliders ready to fight and die on foreign sand and soil hundreds, even thousands of miles from home. Those that survived returned victors. Their wave of euphoria and triumph created the baby boom of the 1950's and led to the most affluent period of modern times.

Fast forward 70 odd years and men are in crisis. A crisis of identity, of physical, emotional and spiritual health. This is compounded by cheap unhealthy foods, limitless availability of pornographic material and 24/7 entertainment. We live in an 'all-you-can-eat' society:

- All you can eat restaurants.
- All you can eat porn.
- All you can eat entertainment.

And for the most part we are gorging ourselves, satisfying our hunger at the feeding trough of Western Civilisation. The result? Obesity, hormone imbalances, infertility and loneliness.
But remember, none of this is your fault, right? You are completely passive in all your choices. Instead you're a victim. Some would even say you're an addict. But addicted to what? Drugs are bad, aren't they?

But these *are* drugs. They are mind and body altering substances that hold you in their grip and never let go. Your drugs are food, porn and computer games. It's convenient to label yourself as a victim because if you have an addiction, you can blame diminished responsibility. You don't have a lack of discipline, YOU HAVE AN ILLNESS. Or do you?

If anyone is to blame for the creeping but intentional feminisation of the father, it's us. We let this happen. We were too busy hunched over our laptops watching porn in the dark, eating Cheetos while we waited for the Xbox to load up. And while we were distracting ourselves, culture shifted. And when we woke up, we'd been labelled as surplus to requirements. Kids these days don't need Dads: look at all those AMAZING SUCCESSFUL SINGLE MOTHERS OUT THERE. AREN'T THEY ALL SO BEAUTIFUL AND AMAZING? Why else would the media glorify the single mother above all other family types? We're sitting eating pizza while the very concept of fatherhood is erased before our eyes.

**The Feminisation of Fatherhood**

Ever since Bonnie Tyler asked, 'Where have all the good men gone?' I've wondered the same thing. Everywhere you look you see the role of men in the family being undermined. Years of cultural conditioning have blind to this. Seeing this truth for the first time is like swallowing the 'red pill'. Kansas is going bye-bye.

The feminisation of fatherhood is like a tap dripping into a bucket. Insignificant at first but leave it overnight and the water overflows. Like the slowly boiling frog, the gradual undermining and feminisation of fatherhood is stealthy and subtle. It may be that you haven't noticed it before but now that I've opened your eyes, can you see it clearly?

If you want to know how society views fathers, follow the news for a week or watch a few modern TV shows and count the number of positive Dad role models. What if you weren't mentally strong enough to discern reality from culturally construed fiction? You would swallow the media's portrayal of fatherhood as truth.

Here's the real truth: Fathers are not the problem. We are the solution. Think about this: when was the last time you met someone with a strong father who turned out to be a mess? Strong, fit fathers have strong, fit sons. My father isn't a tall man, but to me he's a towering giant, characterised by compassion, determination and mental strength. His generation would have preferred prison to some of the demeaning ways Dads are portrayed in our time.

**The Role of The Father on Borrowed Time**

I'm going to go out on a limb and say something completely counter cultural. Are you ready? Here goes: Men and women should have different roles and responsibilities within the family.
30 years ago, this would have been the norm. Instead we've gone a full 180 in the other direction. We've thrown hundreds of metaphorical babies out with gallons of bathwater without even thinking of the consequences. What's the answer? We can ignore and pretend it isn't happening. Or we can open our eyes, harness our confirmation biases and see the hidden signs within the fabric of our culture. We are now living in a time when a man's identity in the family is being eroded to the point where most don't even know what a Dad's job is anymore.

**Don't Be Outraged, Be The Difference**

When you tune into the fact that you are an endangered species as a man, you could feel under threat. Or you could make a conscious decision to be the difference. Anger and outrage take up considerable amounts of energy. Is there a better way?

When you see your role and value being eroded by society, don't become a pathetic outraged victim. Instead, live your life according to the ideals of traditional fatherhood, harnessing your male energy and identity for good. This whole book is about being the difference. That's my father's mission at least. Is it yours?

**Action:** Have you noticed how critical the media is of fathers. Do yourself a favour and limit how much TV and media you consume. Read more books instead (like this one!).

## Pillar 2: Mental - Stress, Fear and the Barriers to Success

Success. I have a mixed relationship with that word. It's not as strong as 'love/hate' but it is a word that gets misused. Spend a few minutes on the internet and you'll find thousands of men and women promising to bring you success. But what does that even mean?

The truth is this: success can mean different things to different people. I like this Oxford dictionary definition:

*"A person or thing that achieves desired aims or attains fame, wealth, etc"*

Those three little words in the middle sum up success - "achieves desired aims". For a long time, I bought into the internet marketers' idea of success: wealth, status, power. But I've come to realise that those things aren't necessarily positive influences and can even be detrimental to overall happiness. Which is what most of us want - to be happy.

How can you be a success as a man and father without being happy? How can you fulfil your father's mission if you feel like a failure all the time?

When you think of happiness, what do you imagine? Is it a long-lost love? A first date? Maybe an idyllic holiday. Or is it something larger, more nebulous. I like to step back and look at the big picture. For me, happiness is about purpose, direction and the people around you. It is also helping others to have better lives. To achieve all of those things constitutes success.

But don't be limited by my view of success or happiness. You are your own person and should have your own aims and purpose in life - some might call it your life's vision.

Here's an extract from one of my favourite books, *Gorilla Mindset* by Mike Cernovich:

*"Think of a goal you'd like to achieve. Maybe it's making more money, or finding a better job, or getting fit. Imagine yourself achieving that goal. Think about where you will be sitting when you reach your goal. What will you look and feel like? Will you be sitting in a large leather chair behind a thick oak desk, or maybe on a hammock in a tropical paradise?"*

Whatever your goal is, I'd encourage you to focus on that goal and believe you can achieve it (also read Gorilla Mindset - it's a great book).

I've subtitled this chapter 'Stress, Fear and the Barriers to Success'. Because if you have a goal, I'm guessing you're not there yet. If you were, would you be looking for answers in this book?

You should be working every day towards your goals. But you know how it goes: some days, you just don't 'feel it'. Imagine your daily energy supply like a bag of sand. At the start of each day the bag is full. But it slowly leaks out as your go through your day until you go to bed. By that stage it's nearly empty - but good news! You'll get a new bag in the morning.

Stress, fear, burnout and a general lack of motivation drain the sand out of your bag more quickly. That's what leaves you flat and lethargic meaning you don't achieve the things you want to. Imagine if you were able to control stress and motivation. Would that make you a better father? Would you be more or less likely to do and achieve all that you want to in life?

This pillar is a focused look at some of the techniques I've used over the years to reduce and eliminate stress, overcome fear and increase my overall motivation. I can only hope that something from these chapters can be useful to you as you continue on your father's mission.

## ***Chapter 1: How to Overcome Fear***

It's a Thursday night and I'm standing wearing nothing but a pair of satin shorts, boxing gloves and shin guards. In about 30 seconds, the Master of Ceremonies is going to call my name. I've trained hard for this. Harder than anything before in my life. But the fear I feel at this point is like nothing I've ever felt before. My opponent, while giving me the best part of 6 pounds, looks in great shape and is experienced. My mouth is dry as I climb into the ring, only vaguely aware of my corner man's reassuring slap on the back. Gloves up, I wait for the referee to begin the fight.

A few years later and I'm standing again, but this time at the open door of a aeroplane. It's pitch black outside and the green glow from the aircraft lights are all I'm using to see now. Fear is etched on my face. The wind rushes past as we cruise in an arc at 120 miles per hour. In about 60 seconds, the dispatcher is going to call my number and I'm going to drive my body out into the aircraft's slipstream.

This fear dwarfs any anxiety I've experienced. The boxing ring feels like a happy memory compared to this. This terror is a crushing weight on my whole body. My eyes are wide as I puff my cheeks. My knees feel like they could give at any moment. '**TWO**', he shouts above the rushing wind. I see a flash of light as I step into nothing.

### **Age brings risk aversion.**

When I look back my life's experiences I can smile. I'm blessed to have been able to be in these positions. It took hard work but many others who would have liked to stand in my position never made it. The thrill of the boxing ring or the rush of the parachute jump are incredible experiences. But I've noticed fear has built as I've grown older. Here's what I mean.

As I get older I'm becoming more risk averse. I have a wife and family now who depend on me being alive and earning for survival and quality of life. Consciously or subconsciously, that thought is in my mind whenever I leave the house. But this fear becomes a problem when it holds you back from experiencing great things or achieving your aims in life.

Fear is a natural and chemical response to perceived risk. It could be before a fight, but it might just as easily be a confrontation at work, a job interview or even 'the talk' with your teenage son.

I chose some extreme examples of personal fear but they are relevant. Why? Because facing fears like these have allowed me to overcome more trivial fears in other contexts. Imagine if you could frame your fears like this:

**"It's not as bad as that time I climbed into a boxing ring with a guy who wanted to hurt me."**

Or

**"This is scary, but nothing compared to that time I jumped out of a light aircraft with a bundled nylon sheet on my back."**

Contextualising your fears with something altogether greater and more fearful makes mundane anxieties easier to cope with and therefore easier to overcome.

**What if you haven't had an experience you can draw on?**

If you've never felt real fear I've got a challenge for you: I want you to do something that really terrifies you. My fear of heights made a parachute jump a joke. Until I did it. Then it was an achievement. What do you need to do right now? Something that REALLY scares you. It could be something as simple as performing at an open mic night or going for a 5k run in public. Or you might want to up the stakes and do a bungee jump or skydive.

But how do you overcome that fear of singing in public, or heights or being laughed at as you run? I've put together the four steps that I've personally used to overcome fear and I'm confident that if you follow them, you'll be that much closer to achieving what you want in life.

**Four Steps to Overcoming Fear**

**1. To Overcome Fear You Must Face Them**

This makes sense but how many times have you had the chance to overcome fear and shied away from it? When I lived overseas, language was a barrier. It took guts to try to speak in the native tribal tongue. People laughed at me but it was important that I could communicate effectively with the locals.

After a while, people began to say that I was 'kind' because I greeted everyone I met in their own language. A little effort on my part went a long way to building bridges with the local tribespeople.
I overcame my fear of speaking another language by doing it. I'd follow the mantra 'Do Something that Scares You Every Day'. That covered a range of activities from taking a motorcycle taxi ride or asking for directions. Sure, you can read helpful articles (like this) or books or go on courses or whatever. But there is no substitute for facing your fears if you're serious about overcoming them.

A lot of people fear job interviews. I used to be that way too. Now I've had countless interviews and I don't fear them anymore. I even enjoy them. Doing the things that scare you bring familiarity and can get rid of fear. I'm pretty scared of heights so jumping out of a plane at 100 mph was about as terrifying as it gets. It was worth it though and I'd do it again in a heartbeat.

**2. Knowledge can Dispel Fear (but not always).**

Knowledge is great. Knowledge can make a man. And Knowledge can allow you to overcome fear. When I stepped into the boxing ring, I had knowledge. I'd been training for weeks and up to 5 hours a day for that moment. I had my sights set on a pro debut the following year. The knowledge and training kicked in as soon as the bell rang for round 1. I felt calm and in control because I'd spent time gaining the knowledge required to compete at that level.

Jumping out of an aircraft is different. I've done it several times now and feel fear every time. The outcome is always a little uncertain so I'm thinking about what I have to do on exiting the plane, what to do if something goes wrong and so on. I've spoken to friends who do free fall and BASE jumping and have hundreds of jumps under their belt. They still feel fear. It's natural. The question is not whether you feel fear, but if you can overcome it.

**3. Use Gorilla Mindset Techniques**

I used to struggle to cope with fear and anxiety. Not so long ago I would be a complete mess under any kind of pressure or prolonged stress. When I started using the techniques within *Gorilla Mindset* (mentioned earlier) that all changed. Self-talk is one of these techniques in which you use positive language in your personal thoughts to get out of negative ways of thinking.

This is linked with another technique called being 'In the moment' where you use active meditation to be hyper aware of your surroundings. For example, I'd be thinking to myself: 'I'm sitting in a plane, I can see rectangles and squares in the panels. I'm looking out of the window and I can see geometric fields, trees and buildings'… and so on.

This annihilates fear as you can't focus on two things at the same time. Don't believe me? Try it now. Imagine you are somewhere or doing something that terrifies you. Feel the fear coursing through your body. The stop and focus on where you are, what you're doing. You're back in your house or on the bus, reading this book. The words look crisp and black on the screen. Your breathing is slow and controlled. Can you still feel the fear? I didn't think so.

## 4. Buying Immunity from Fear

Overcoming fear became more of a challenge when I became a Dad. I didn't particularly want to do crazy 'out there' stuff in case I died in an horrific accident and my family had to go on welfare to get by. So I got life insurance. (No, this isn't a joke). This is a straight-up genuine way that I started to cope with and ultimately overcome fear. I got life insurance that covered me for all the mad stuff I wanted to do (parachuting anyone?). It was expensive but it worked.

Because when I'm standing in the door of a plane I'm about to jump out of, I'm thinking 'If the worst happens, my family will be OK.' And not 'Maybe I shouldn't be doing this.' So often you put barriers in your way. 'What if I die?' is a big obstacle. Or is it? What if you answered your own question with an answer like this: "If I die my family will be upset but they will be financially well looked after and know that I died doing something that I love." Answering your own question removes some of the worst fear.

Should you seek out near death experiences? That's up to you. Whatever activity you're engaged in, be ready with a response. When that voice in your head questions if you're good enough, fit enough or experienced enough, you'll know what to say back.

## Overcome Fears - My One Piece of Advice

If I had to pick one piece of advice from this whole chapter, it would be this:

**Find the thing that scares you and do it.**

It might not be planes or heights or anything major but if you're scared of it, you need to overcome it or risk living an unfulfilled life of regret. Will that type of existence lead you to where you want to be? Or will it hinder you. I'm writing this book right now and it scares me. What if no one reads it? What if they do but think it's awful, pretentious rubbish? It would be easier for me not to write a book.

And because it scares me, I want to do it. Because I know that I will overcome my fear of writing a book by (you guessed it) writing a book! What is the thing that scares you most of all? Seek it out and overcome it. You'll waltz through lesser fears like they don't even exist.

## *Chapter 2: Finding the Motivation to Succeed*

Let me begin this chapter with a personal question. How motivated do you feel right now? Give yourself a score of 1-10. Imagine a score of '1' being the least motivated you've ever been in your life like the time you had flu and couldn't even get out of bed. Whereas a 10 would be when you were firing on all cylinders - everything was great and you leapt out of bed every day ready to make a difference.

Right now, I'm feeling good - I'm writing this book, my other interests are going well and I'm learning new skills like basic web design and coding so I'd give myself a 7 or an 8. This is indicative of times in my life when I've felt extremely motivated and achieved a lot as a result. I've soared on the crests of multiple accomplishments. I've made constant improvements which led to the fulfilment of goals. This motivation has often lasted years when everything has gone great. My motivation levels have been phenomenal. Other times I've felt flat. This flatness can last for days, weeks, months, even years. I have waded through demotivated fugs where I considered my life as being one big Groundhog Day. In February 2015, I was going through one of these times. I posted something on the internet I'll never forget:

*"I used to walk through the city and smell opportunity. Now all I can smell is stale coffee and broken dreams."*

When I tweeted this, I meant it. I felt that there was no opportunity left for me. All the excitement I had felt as a younger man had dissipated like smoke in a hurricane. When I first moved to the city I remember the rush of the morning commute. I would get the subway to the centre of the financial district, riding up the escalator in my new suit and shined shoes. I felt like the master of my own destiny. But that faded as the grind of work, office politics and crushing debt kicked in. I was a prisoner to my own perceived limitations.

As a Dad, I've fallen even further that I would have before. It's easy to get stuck in a rut of work, bath times, bed times and weekends. Whole months can pass in which you feel like you've achieved nothing.

Lack of motivation symptoms for me can include:

- Putting effort into banal and pointless activities e.g. boxed set marathons
- A lack of discipline in other areas such as fitness and diet
- A creeping acceptance of the status quo
- Writing garbage tweets (see above)
- A scarcity mindset

But what about the times when I'm on an up. What characterises these times? What if you could harness the energies that go into those 'up' times to push through the inevitable negativity of the low? I fully believe it's possible to create an environment where these following three factors can be encouraged and replicated. Here's how:

### 1. The Desire for Success

We all want success. No one starts their day inviting failure. But what does the desire for success look like? I can think back to times in my life when I desired success, not in business, but in sport. In my mid-twenties, I was moving towards fighting professionally in Muay Thai (Thai boxing).

As I built up through the levels my coaches had put in place for me to get there, I became more and more focused. Everything was about that goal. My eating, sleeping and training all pointed towards what I wanted to achieve. I would train for up to five hours per day, often to the point of exhaustion. I sparred with the top pro fighters in the gym and even a future UFC pro to experience what it was like to get hit hard. Some days I would become so battered and bruised from sparring I would pop prescription strength painkillers just so I could train the following day. I even remember walking carefully around the house, worried about bumping into furniture and injuring myself in a freak accident. When a snowstorm shut public transport links, I walked for miles across the city so I could get to the gym.

In addition to this, I imagined and visualised every aspect of my upcoming fights: how it would feel when I walked in, how it would feel to win, how it would feel to be bruised, bloodied but victorious. The desire to succeed was so powerful that it drove me to improve - to be faster, fitter and stronger.

Have you ever felt like this before? Maybe you were studying for an exam or preparing for a job interview. Perhaps you were reading all the books you could on fatherhood so that you'd be the model dad? Visualise that sense of motivation, that desire. What did it feel like? Bring that sense of desire into your everyday life, into the seemingly mundane tasks of working hard and being a good father and husband.

**2. The Fear or Failure**

Fear of failure is not something that comes to mind when you talk about motivation.
You would struggle to find a motivational speaker or life coach who gets his clients to imagine themselves failing. And then use that to motivate them.

But that's exactly what I've done in the past. I've used the fear of failure to force me to succeed.
As with desiring success, I've imagined what failure would feel like. What would it feel like to let myself down? To let my family down and be a laughing stock as people laugh behind their sleeves at me. I've purposely gone to these darkest places to draw strength from them. I tell myself that death is preferable to failure. I don't mean it but if I can convince myself that's truth, I'm more likely to succeed.

When going through selection to become a member of the British airborne forces, I got sick before the last few selection events. I struggled on but eventually reported to the medical centre hoping I could be taken off the course. I felt like a failure and had to wait nearly a year before I could go through the process again.

In that time I went deep into my own mind. I looked my own sense of failure straight in the eyes. I remembered what it was like to tell the hopeful faces of friends and family that I'd failed. I remembered the awkward silence as the NCO drove me back to my unit headquarters. I stored all that pain and used it to motivate me on the dark, sleet filled mornings as I pounded the pavements and completed pull-ups on frozen playground climbing frames.

The pain of failing, of knowing you could have tried harder and succeeded is unimaginable. I pity you a little if you've never felt this. It's a huge life lesson. I've used the recollection of that feeling to succeed and overcome. It's a hard route and isn't for everyone. But it works for me. Maybe it can work for you?

Try this: Think about a time when you failed and were disappointed. How did you feel. Horrible? Good. Now think about something you want to achieve. Imagine failing and feeling those feelings again. It hurts doesn't it? You don't want to fail so use that feeling to motivate you do succeed. To do more and be more towards your goals.

### 3. A Faith in Something Bigger

My faith is a big motivator for me. I'm a Christian and have a desire to do more and be more that comes from my faith. I find it hard to consider how someone of no faith can be motivated if they don't believe in a higher purpose and a bigger spiritual picture.

I'm not here to preach. There are plenty of people and books that will do that for me. But I hope that you do believe in something and have a faith that what we do on this earth matters. And if you do, I hope that you can use that to motivate you to do more and to be more than you are today.

My faith goes deep within me and my psyche. I've drawn on it in times of emotional need for comfort and motivation. Studies even show that religious athletes perform better than non-religious ones. Clearly not all faiths can be right about the details of their religion but there is an undeniable benefit from believing in a Higher Power.

**Motivation - Harness the Energy**

If I had to summarise this chapter, I'd say that the way to 'find' motivation is to find a way to harness energy. Using the desire for success, the fear of failure and the belief in something bigger has given me incredible motivation where I've achieved so much more than I could have ever imagined.

To get that motivation for yourself you will need to go deep within your own experiences and draw that power out from within your mind. Desire is powerful and if channelled correctly can bring incredible results.

Drawing energy and power from a Higher Source (God) can also yield big results in your life. I believe that He wants good things for me and for me to succeed, not because it makes me look good but because it reflects well on Him.

Clearly, I don't have all the answers. But I've come a long way since that negative tweet in 2015. Being motivated means having the drive and desire to achieve what you want in life. Use your life experiences for good and you can achieve great things in family, career and relationships.

### *Chapter 3: How to Deal With Burnout*

If you don't know what burnout is, it probably means you've never suffered from it. Imagine a persistent feeling of being overloaded and overwhelmed. It's a feeling of being unable to escape.

You are so busy that you can't even begin to think about what task you need to do next. The kids are fighting in the other room while you are trying to plan for your next day at work.

Meanwhile your partner is giving you a hard time about not being more attentive and all you want to do is run away and live the life of a hermit. You need to take action. You need to be released from this vortex of anxiety and fatigue.

You may have your own definition of burnout but this is mine:

*Burnout is a feeling of persistent overload and overwhelming responsibility*

Burnout is the creeping feeling that you can't escape from your surroundings and obligations coupled with a fatigue that can't be satisfied by mere sleep. In my experience, burnout is something that builds slowly over time. You gradually take on more and more responsibilities until you're at breaking point.

When I lived among the expat community in Uganda, burnout was rife. The pressures of schooling, working and generally living in a different culture drains even the strongest individual. I saw resilient men and women melt into a haze of mental and physical health problems.

Now we know what burnout is, how do you deal with it? I don't mean 'how do you cope day to day?', I mean beat burnout back into the back of beyond from whence it came. I'd recommend using a big hefty metaphorical stick if you have to. The point is this: you shouldn't be burned out. It's just not an acceptable state to be in. Being told to 'Man

Up' is poor advice given by men and women who know nothing about you. You'll need to take drastic action starting from RIGHT NOW if you are going to triumph over it.

Beating burnout with this four-step process has worked well for me. I might even say 'wonders'. Now whenever I feel like I'm getting a little burned out, I'll look over these steps and take any action I need. If you want to know what they are, keep reading.

**Step 1: Declutter your life**

One of the major factors in my own burnout was that I was doing too much. I was engaged in too many extra-curricular activities as well as trying to hold down a demanding job, a long commute and a medium intensity fitness regime. I became anxious and even panicky at times and this spilled into my interactions with other people. That's when burnout becomes a real problem: when it affects your relationships with others, especially your kids.

So, I quit. I didn't do it as a knee-jerk reaction but as a measured response. I resigned a number of voluntary positions, I ended freelance and weekend work and focused on going to my day job, staying healthy and being a family man. People didn't like it. When people are used to you being around so that they can load responsibility on you they like it. When you say, 'I've had enough and you'll have to find someone else' things can get ugly. *People who are used to using you don't like it when you quit.*

If those closest to you can't deal with the fact that you need a break, do they really have your best interests at heart? Maybe you need to think more about whether they are the kind of people you want in your life longer term. Over demanding and manipulative people shouldn't really be in your inner circle if you can help it.

Try saying 'No' to everything for three months. That's a 'No' to the opening at your son's football club coaching team. 'No' to joining the

PTA/Residents' Association/Sailing Club. 'No' to working late. My weakness was voluntary roles. I used to take on new responsibilities thinking 'It's only one day a month'. But if you do that for four different things, you've got an extra commitment every single week.

In the co-authored book '*The Power of No*' James and Claudia Altucher's take on this is simple. If you say 'No' to others demanding your time, you're actually saying 'yes' to a healthier and happier you, better relationships and a more abundant life. Is it time you said 'No' so that you could say 'Yes'?

**Step 2. De-clutter Your Relationships**

Having to deal with negative and draining people is challenging at the best of times. But doing it when you're feeling overwhelmed is near suicidal. Don't stand for people who want to take, take, take from you all the time. If you're not strong enough to meet their needs, give them a wide berth.

The same goes with Social Media – why spend hours scrolling through pages of your ex-school friends who have made a complete mess of their lives. Do some hard-core 'Unfriending'. You'll feel better – I guarantee it. About once a year I have a full audit of my Facebook page, severing contact with people that I neither know or care about anymore. I've also found it useful to keep off Social Media around bedtimes. I have to be strict with myself and have my phone on flight mode or I'd be too tempted to have a quick peek at what everyone's been up to. Try this: put your phone on airplane mode when you go upstairs to bed. You might find you end up having more sex or get more reading done.

Stay away from negative talk and gossip in the office. Did you ever leave a gossip session feeling better about yourself or your job? You'd be surprised how these negative bitching sessions can affect your energy levels and contribute to your sense of burnout. Get out at lunch time – go for a walk, sit in the park or pop down to the driving range for thirty minutes.

**Step 3: De-clutter Your Home**

This should seem obvious, right? If your house or flat or apartment is in a mess, how can you hope to have an ordered life? So, have a clear out. One thing that struck me recently is this: It's amazing how much stuff you *don't* need. Think of all the junk in your house – CDs you don't listen to, DVDs you never watch, books you read, clothes that don't fit. Now imagine your house with all that stuff gone. Better isn't it?

What's more you can often get money for these things. Here in the UK, you can sell old clothes and books to different merchants. You could have a garage sale or sell your stuff on a website like Gumtree (a UK version of Craigslist). If you were feeling benevolent you could even give it away to charity. Every year, I clear all the junk out of the garage. I sell what can be sold and recycle or bin everything else. It's a difficult and time-consuming job but is well worth it for a tidy and simplified existence.

Don't stop with physical things though. Can you declutter your finances? Recently I consolidated all of my investments from 4 different providers into one. Not only do I have more control, but it's given me peace of mind knowing that I have easy access to my money if I need it. Can you stop any subscriptions for services that you don't need? Is that magazine subscription just creating a headache for storing all the back issues? Look to live without clutter and you'll give burnout a big ol' body swerve.

**Step 4: De-clutter Your Inbox**

This takes real discipline and determination but it's time to claim back your inbox. Like most Dads it's probably stuffed full of newsletters, special offer emails and other sales junk. In fact, when was the last time you got an email from an *actual* person? Try this: Go 'unsubscribe' crazy – even if that means unsubscribing from the This Dad Does newsletter. If that's what you have to do to beat burnout, then you have my full support.

Junk and spam email is a bit like a Gremlin – it's really hard to kill (using a blender isn't advised). You'll probably have to go back and have an unsubscribe-blitz every few months. But having a near empty inbox is worth it every time.

**Don't Suffer Alone**

Hopefully this four-step process will lead you down the path of escaping Dad Burnout. Thinking that you have to 'Man Up' or 'Snap Out of It' is not going to cut it. You need to take practical steps now. Decluttering your life through relationships, possessions and how you use the internet will all help.

But what if it still feels like it's too much. One thing you should never do is bottle it all up inside. Speak to someone, preferably a peer or a member of your Dad Network if you have one. If you don't, I'll tell you how in the next chapter. They may suggest you see a counsellor or your doctor which may be a smart move. If you have a partner, you should also tell her.

Life is busy, but that doesn't mean you need to feel burned out. Know the signs and know what to do if it happens again. Next time burnout comes knocking, you'll be ready.

**Action:** Make a list of all your extra-curricular activities. Are there any that you should drop? Have you taken on too much? Take some time to trim your commitments. Your future self will thank you.

## *Chapter 4: Build Your Dad Network*

Networks are important. Whether they're at work, at church, at your sports team's supporters club – having a network of likeminded people can have multiple benefits. But how important is it to have a network of other Dads? And if it's important, what benefits is it going to bring?

What do I mean by a 'Dad Network'? Here's my definition:

*"A Dad Network is a community of likeminded Dads who challenge each other to be better in all areas of life."*

If you're anything like me, you go out of your way to surround yourself with positive people. When it comes to being a Dad, there's no difference. I'm privileged to have an extensive network of other Dads. Many of them are successful in business, fitness, sport, media and have good track records as Dads. We meet up, do stuff together and bounce ideas and knowledge off each other. Some are friends from University, some from my church, some I met through other hobbies and interests I have. It takes effort to stay in touch and up to date but the benefits are worth it.

I also have a growing network of likeminded Dads through my website ThisDadDoes.com. Because I write about the things I value, Dads who think the same way are drawn to me. But it's a mutually beneficial relationship. I've made some great friends through the internet and social media and had my views of the world and fatherhood challenged in all different directions.

What are the benefits of a Dad Network? When tough times come, there is nothing particularly heroic about going your own. Even the US Navy SEALS need their buddies with them to get the job done, right? So why are you any different as you embark on the father's mission? If you are going to be mentally tough and able to cope with the stresses and strains of fatherhood, do you really think it's going to be a solo effort?

The truth is you need others around you. These should preferably be older and wiser Dads that can give you advice, a man-hug or even just tell you that you're an idiot. A lot of my Dad network are experienced in business and finance and can easily give good money advice. Others have excelled in sport or fitness up to a professional level and have great insight and tips for training, and nutrition.

Some in my Dad Network have seen tough times in relationships, money and generally in family life. They've lost jobs, wives and seen their lives fall apart and have come out the other end. Those are the Dads I want in my corner.

This is all well and good if you have a Dad Network already. But what if you don't. Or you moved away to somewhere new and need to start from scratch. How can you build your Dad Network from the ground up? Keep reading for my top Dad Network building tips.

**How to get your Dad Network Started**

If you don't have a network of Dads, *make one.* Kids sports clubs are an obvious place to pick up other Dads. Get talking to them after training or before or during games or competitions. You already have something in common i.e. your kids' athletic skills so you have a starting point for conversations. Once you're on first name terms, invite them round for a barbecue or a Friday night beer.

A great place to meet and talk to other Dads is a toddler play group. As a Dad, you will almost always be in a minority and Dads gotta stick together. You'll make connections easily. Be intentional about your friendships – you want this relationship to be mutually beneficial. A line from a Soul Asylum song is 'Nothing attracts a crowd like a crowd' and it's true. If three Dads is a crowd, you'll quickly attract others into your group and before you know it, you'll have an extensive network of likeminded male role models.

Social media, especially Twitter is a good place to meet and connect with other Dads. If you get on well, why not arrange a Skype chat. If you live close by, why not arrange a meet up. Look for blogs, websites or forums that suit your interests. There are groups of Dads that are interested in the same thing as you - even if that's something as obscure as Japanese Pro-Wrestling. It's never been easier to connect with other people than in our current times.

**A Strong Dad Network builds Strong Dads**

Are you now convinced that you need a network of likeminded Dads? Yes I used the word *need*. You are wired to desire male company. Too much time with your wife and kids will drive you crazy. You need time to just be a man with other men every now and then. How you do that is up to you. If you like golf, play golf. If you are into gardening, join a horticultural club. If eating contests are your thing, choose another activity…

Imagine this: If you put a brick on the ground, what do you have? A brick. If you put lots of bricks on top of each other in the right way, add some mortar, and you have a strong wall that will last for decades. It's the same with your network.

Or if you fire up the barbecue and get it nice and hot, but remove one of the red-hot coals and set it alone, what happens? It goes cold and dies out. It needs the mutual energy of the other hot coals to fulfil it's purpose - cooking your perfect steaks.

If your Dad Network is strong – you meet up regularly and invest your time in making it stronger, you will reap the benefits. Being a Dad is tough and it's going to get harder. But if your strength comes from those around you as well as within you'll come out on top.

**Action:** Plan how you're going to make your Dad Network stronger. Or if you don't have one, plan how you're going to start one. Set yourself a deadline of 6 months to get it done by.

## Pillar 3: Spirituality and Self Control

Is it strange to be writing a whole section on spirituality? You might be thinking so. In fact, it's something I've barely written about before. But I do consider myself to be a spiritual guy. So, if I'm writing a book about the tools that Dads need to fulfil their mission in the world then I'd be dishonest to myself and you the reader if I left out any suggestion of the spiritual.

Spirituality, and in particular the Christian faith, has been a central part of my identity for so long that I can barely remember a time that I didn't call myself a Christian.

But I appreciate that you may be reading this with a different take on faith. Or even be of no faith. You'll be pleased to know that I'm not going to go all out to convince you that I'm right and you're wrong. But I am going to have an honest discussion about the merits of a spiritual life.

The spiritual aspect to life doesn't have to start and finish with a major world religion. I'm not interested in mixing my Christian faith with any kind of new thinking or cherry picking other parts of the religions I like. The flipside of this is that there is powerful value in living a more spiritual life that includes meditation, prayer and control of breathing and the senses.

What can you expect over the next few short chapters? I'm going to start by giving an overview of religion and why it still has relevance for modern fathers. I'll also look at improving your breathing and cold exposure. We'll also look at self-control and how you can overcome something as self-destructive as drinking or pornography usage. I bet you're glad you didn't skip over this section now, right?

What does spirituality have to do with a father's mission? And what will we have achieved by the end of these next few pages? Will I have converted you to the Christian faith? Probably not. But I hope to have convinced you that spirituality matters and will continue to matter on your father's mission.

## *Chapter 1: Why Spirituality Doesn't Suck – Religion for Modern Dads*

What does spirituality have to do with a father's mission? Strangely this chapter has been one of the hardest for me to write. I say strangely because I'm a pretty religious guy. But I want to make this book relevant for you the reader. What's the point of reading a book like this if it's not going to help you?

I've spent a while thinking about how I should approach this subject. How do I explain why I think spirituality is a key aspect of being a father? I appreciate that I may well be writing this to you as an agnostic or even atheistic reader. If so, I've written this chapter with you in mind – not to convince you of the truth of my personally held beliefs – but to persuade you that a spiritual life has value in your mission as a Dad.

The best way for me to do this is from my own experience. And that adds another challenge: where to start? Hopefully by the time we're done you'll at least understand where I'm coming from and know that for someone who is in touch with the spiritual side of life there is a net gain in sharing this with your kids.

### The Indoctrination Paradox

I've heard arguments against bringing your kids up as religious. These arguments seem to centre around the fact that this is brainwashing on a domestic scale and therefore is bad.

However, these same opponents of parental conditioning of kids never seem to take the same stern line with parents who raise their kids to be vegetarians, CND activists, socialists or eco-warriors (all lifestyles which are based on values and beliefs). The truth is this: if you're doing a good job of raising your kids you can't help but inspire some of your personally held values into their lives as they grow.

Whether they reject those values at a later date is up to them (like my friend who ate his first slice of bacon on his 16th birthday after being raised as a vegetarian – he loved it). But you shouldn't feel ashamed of communicating something that is of value to your children.

Here's a good example: I love soccer. My team is Raith Rovers – a little Scottish club that could attract 2000 fans on a good day. I'll always support them and when my son is old enough, we'll go to games together. He may grow up to be a Raith Rovers fan. Or he may reject them and support St Johnstone or even Inverness. That will be his decision. But I'll take him to the games for as long as he will go with me.

The same applies for my Christian faith. It will be a major aspect of my children's upbringing. Those who think this is sinister have a deeper agenda than just the way I raise my kids. And they almost certainly don't have your children's best interests at heart.

**A Brief History of my Christian Upbringing**

"Do you bash the Bible?"

How was I to answer this question? It was being posed to me by two older boys who had crossed the street to confront me and were now blocking my path. I was carrying my euphonium (a bit like a large French horn - very heavy) on the way back from band practice. I had a split second to think of a response.

"Aye, every night."

Not true – but then they didn't even know what they were asking me. 'Bible Basher' probably rolled off their tongues so it sounded clever to them.

"Well bash this then!" One said as he swung a plastic folder full of school books in my unguarded face, breaking my nose for the first time.

Stunned, I walked on towards home with blood starting drip down my lip mixing with hot tears of shame.

Growing up as the Pastor's kid in a Scottish Council housing estate (think US projects without the guns) felt tough as a kid. Most of my neighbours were my father's parishioners. There was always an unseen pressure on me to behave in a certain way. But on balance it was a happy and privileged childhood. School books to the face aside, my religious background was more blessing than judgement.

Aged fourteen I decided to own my faith and live life as a Christian. I was the only one of my friends who was religious which was the way it stayed until I left school at seventeen. Interestingly there were others at my school who called themselves 'Christians' but they also seemed to be good at getting 'like totally wasted' at the local rugby club socials or being caught in compromising positions in the janitor's closet (not with the janitor, thankfully).

Although my life has never been that of a saint, my Christian upbringing and faith has been a consistent, steady leaning post throughout my life. It gives me direction, hope and a way of understanding the universe. A few years ago, I even considered making it my career, going back to University to study Theology with one eye on becoming ordained as a pastor. In the end, my life took a different turn and I don't have any regrets. But my spiritual journey remains a strong part of my identity.

But what if you are a sceptic to all of this? You may be thinking something like this:

"Pfft, I have science, what do I need GOD for??"

It's been a convenient tool of militant atheism to pitch science against religion as being incompatible 'cuz Creationism'. What they won't tell you is that many prominent scientists were professing Christians (Sir Isaac Newton anyone?). I've got a science degree and found nothing in my lessons of geology, molecular biology or ecology that disproved anything taught in the Bible. The mistake that some Christians make is taking the Bible and using it as something it wasn't meant for. For example, they might use it as a science manual, or a barometer to interpret current events as being the harbingers of the end times.

Here's why using the Bible as your geology textbook is flawed: Most of the Bible was written in the early to late bronze age. While the people of that time were intelligent, a holy book that described the Universe in the way that we understand it would have blown their minds! Can you imagine sitting down with your bronze age self and explaining about atoms, matter and the Big Bang? They would either believe you to be a sorcerer, insane or both.

But there is another side to this. Science falls short in helping you towards understanding the universe and how you fit into it. Science gives you the 'how' but not the 'why?'. Belief that the entire universe is a series of completely random events is a bigger jump than understanding that there is an all-powerful Benefactor and Creator. If such a being exists, he is the Father of the Universe. Which is pretty scary but cool at the same time?

But how does your Spirituality fit into your mission as a father?

My own experience of having a religious father is a positive one. My father is a deeply compassionate and selfless person willing to talk and listen to anyone. When a local group of Islamic elders needed a space to pray, he let them use his living room as a temporary measure.

He would spend hours caring for the mentally ill and those trapped in addiction. His ministry dealt regularly with death and the dying. Growing up, he always had time for me and would be ready to give guidance and advice as needed. His relaxed approach to fatherhood allowed me to become my own man and ultimately choose Christianity for myself.

My childhood benefited from a spiritual home which is why I cannot imagine raising my kids in anything else. In practice, this means teaching my kids how to pray, acts of mercy, about the Bible and of course other religions.

But now I reach a problem. If you're a religious father, I know you're nodding along to what you've read in agreement. But if you're not and are agnostic or a passive atheist you may be a little bemused or confused by what you've just read. How can you cultivate a spiritual home when you don't believe any religion or have an understanding of the spiritual? There are a number of things you can do to help yourself and your spiritual journey. These are:

- Learn all you can about the spiritual realm world religions. Have an open mind and be prepared to understand that religion has value where it is taught faithfully and without political agenda.

- Read spiritual texts and understand ancient mythology.

- Be prepared to teach your kids about the spiritual through your own words and actions. I've known many who have walked away from religion because their well-meaning parents focused on harsh discipline rather than the selfless love of Christianity.

- Take time to be more connected with the spiritual – whether you understand that to be God, a life force or the Universe. I've had deeply spiritual experiences climbing mountains, meditating and doing Wim Hof breathing – a type of deep respiration that promotes peace and control of the mind and body.

Approach with an open mind and you may find more answers than you knew you had questions. I've valued the extra layer of a spiritual home – won't your children feel the same way?

**Finding Value in the Spiritual Home**

In this chapter, I've wanted to convey to you the value of a spiritual home and childhood that I've experienced first-hand. If you had the same experience, you know what I'm talking about. If you had a negative religious experience as a child, I feel bad – because you were miss-sold something which, if done right, can fill you with wonder and an incredible sense of peace and purpose. If you weren't raised in a spiritual home I envy you because now you have a clean slate with which to explore and be amazed by what I know you will find.

## *Chapter 2: The Power of Breathing and Cold Exposure*

I start the long trudge back to my car. The Scottish hillside has been a wet, slithery wasteland for the past 8 hours and I'm soaked to the skin. As I reach my vehicle parked up on vantage point high above the valley I'm relieved. At this height, the temperature has dropped to just above freezing. The rain falls mixed with part melted chunks of snow. I take off my sopping jacket and shirt at the car boot stripping down to my bare chest. I stand for a while, revelling in the feeling of the air and wind against my skin. I control my breathing to prevent the sharp inhalation that cold exposure can bring. I'm alive and I feel everything.

Have I completely lost my mind? What would possess you to stand half naked, arms outstretched in a Scottish winter landscape? Is this madness? Or is there something else happening here - something deeper, something more profound. A lost connection with an ancestral heritage and the elements?

### Breathe. Just Breathe.

I had never heard of Wim Hof until April 2016. Hof is a Dutchman who has made a name for himself through insane feats of physical endeavour. He's climbed Everest without oxygen and regularly exposes himself to freezing water, sub-zero temperatures and even infectious diseases. His motivation? To explore the limits of the human body and mind. If anyone is living on the edge, it's Hof. And he has followers - thousands of them.

Hof has dedicated his life to his craft. His techniques have been compiled into a training programme called the Wim Hof method. There are a range of courses and even a smartphone app. I'd recommend visiting his website for more details (https://www.wimhofmethod.com/).

But I didn't write this chapter to sell you on some online course (which I hear is very good). I've learned some of Wim Hof's techniques and put them into practice. They can add real value to your life as a man and as a father. When I say, 'add value' it sounds like a sales pitch or something you'd hear me say in a job interview. But before I get into what I mean, let me summarise what I've learned from experience and from the Wim Hof method that will help you in your father's mission.

As you embark on your father's mission and become a Dad who does more, you will be looking to improve yourself. One of the ways you can do this is through personal and physical discipline. We'll cover physical discipline more in the final chapter so let's think more about personal discipline and self-control. While spirituality takes a great deal of personal discipline to develop, there is an intersection between the more mental aspect of spirituality and the physical aspect of personal self-control. When you think about self-control, you probably imagine resisting temptation of the office cake. Or jumping straight out of bed instead of hitting that snooze button.

But what if there was a deeper level of self-control where you could **physically re-programme** yourself to feel and even behave differently? Author and cartoonist Scott Adams calls this the *moist robot hypothesis*. The meaning behind this is, when it comes down to it, you are just a big squidgy, wet, programmable machine. Robots behave based on input which they then process and creates an output. Therefore, if you imagine yourself as a robot, you can control how you feel and behave by changing what goes in.

What if you could re (or pre) programme yourself just by controlling the way you breathe. Sounds crazy, doesn't it? And if you've never done any breathing exercises you'll be unaware of how much breathing impacts on how you feel and react. The first part of this is being in-tune with how you feel in a physical sense. What do you feel right now? As I'm writing this I'm listening to some Vivaldi (I love classical music to write to). I'm relaxed and my breathing is slow and controlled. I feel a little anxious from the double espresso I drank 20 minutes ago - the caffeine is kicking in. Otherwise I'm at peace as my fingers glide over the keys.

But imagine if an intruder broke down my back door as I was writing. My breathing would change very quickly in response to the threat. Even the thought of that scenario made my breathing a little shorter and shallower! That's because your body has a well-developed response to threat whereby adrenaline is produced which allows you to 'fight or flight'. That's great if you're being chased by a lion or a musk ox. Not so good for the office cubicle or your kids' bath times.

What if you were able to become more conscious of how you breathe and could adjust it at will. You'd feel a lot calmer in those non-lion-chasing-but-otherwise-quite-stressful situations you inevitably come across in life. It takes time to become more in tune with your physical state but a good place to start is to take time during the day to examine your state - how do you feel, how are you sitting and most importantly - how are you breathing? I recommend reading *Gorilla Mindset* by Mike Cernovich for some excellent exercises for state control and mindfulness.

Breathing exercises are a great way to learn how to control your breathing and become more aware of how you breathe. Wim Hof's take on breathing is pretty extreme:

*"We're always breathing, yet we're mostly unaware of its tremendous potential. Heightened oxygen levels hold a treasure trove of benefits: more energy, reduced stress levels, and an augmented immune response to swiftly deal with pathogens."*

These aren't wild claims from a crazy Dutchman either. Hof has tested his theories under controlled scientific conditions and baffled medical professionals with his ability to manipulate his physical body far beyond the limitations of regular guys like you and me.

Hof advocates a breathing exercise where you breathe deeply for a while and then exhale fully - and rest without breathing in - for as long as possible. It can get pretty intense once you learn the techniques and is very relaxing. I've even experienced deep euphoria during these sessions. Once, before a job interview, I breathed in this way and felt instantly calmer and in control as I walked into the interview room. Often Hof says, 'Just breathe!' as if we've forgotten how to do it properly which we probably have. If you learn to breath properly and can control that breathing at times of high stress you'll be more in control and feel healthier. You'll have changed your moist robot's programming which will make you more effective as a Dad.

**Left Out in the Cold**

Look around you. Where are you right now? You might be on a train or at home. Maybe you're in bed or having a break at the office. Either way, you're probably comfortably warm. I'm writing this in a well-insulated house with the heating on. I'm also wearing a sweater. I'm not sweating but I'm a long way from being cold. But is this the best way for you to be all the time?

There are numerous studies that show cold exposure to have beneficial health benefits - both physical and mental. Much of this is connected to improvements in circulation. When coupled with deep breathing and focus that Wim Hof and others advocate, cold exposure can have dramatic effects on mood, healthy and recovery from exercise. A 2008 study showed cold showers to act in the same way as antidepressant drugs by stimulating nerve endings and increasing brain activity.

Next time you have a shower, try turning the dial down towards the colder end just a little for the last 30 seconds. After a few days of doing this, make it a little colder each week until you're able to stand under a fully cold stream. Keeping breathing controlled and steady will help you feel comfortable and in control. After a while your body will become used to the sensation and you will begin to enjoy that short while in the cold (trust me!).

I've personally seen the healing effects of water of varying temperatures first hand. In my early 20's I suffered a bad snowboarding injury to my knee. My leg was swollen and I was in a lot of pain. After visiting a

Swiss spa and rotating between a saline (salt-water) pool, steam room and cold plunge pool I regained mobility as well as reduced pain and swelling.

**Don't Go With What You Know**

Intense breathing and cold exposure sound pretty hokey. But only if you've never tried them. It's unwise to dismiss these things out of hand when the science *and* anecdotal evidence backs up the value of breathing exercises *ala* Wim Hof. The weight of scientific research into cold exposure should have you running a bath and reaching for the bag of ice too. If you're living an active intense life as a man and a father, it's imperative that you take care of your physical, mental and spiritual state. Just being alone for fifteen minutes to focus on your breathing can be the difference between a good and a really crappy day.

Build yourself up gradually, starting by focusing on how you breathe and in what situation and fiddling with that shower dial. You may just be surprised at the positive results.

## *Chapter 3: The Power of Self Control and Self Denial*

*"He is no fool who loses what he cannot keep, to gain what he cannot lose."* - Jim Elliot

Are you the kind of father who loses control easily? You have lofty ideas of living a disciplined life where you live a mentally and physically healthy life and do good deeds for others. But when push comes to shove, you're just as weak as the next man. If this sounds like you then we're in good company. I'm one of the weakest people I know when it comes to self-control. But this comes with a caveat. Over the years I've learned how to deal with my most self-destructive habits so that they don't affect my life in the way that they used to. These two self-destructive past times were:

- Heavy drinking
- Pornography usage and engagement

Sound familiar? Or maybe you have a different set of weaknesses - food, women, even drugs (I'm not here to judge.) Whatever it is, you have the power to overcome these weaknesses. For me, my faith is a big motivator to becoming a better man and father. That gives me the 'why', but not always the 'how'. That's why I've selected my two biggest and most harmful vices to show you what can be done when you make real change and commitment in your life. Prepare to be challenged by what you read.

My writing, especially on pornography, comes with a warning. If you are sensitive or don't want the details, skip this chapter.

### How to Beat Self Destructive Drinking

I went to University when I was 17. I was 20 when I left with two things: A Bachelor's degree and a drink problem.

It started with occasional nights out and quickly escalated into week long binges where I was drunk or hungover more than I was sober. A few times I made myself ill to the point when I look back now I'm surprised I didn't end up in hospital. Other times I blacked out and had no recollection of how I got home. Sometimes I would wake in the morning with cuts on my hands, unsure of where I'd hurt myself or why.

I went out for drinks for my 20th birthday – I remember nothing after about 8.30pm apart from a 10 second flashback stumbling around in the snow trying to find my way home. Nights like this could have ended differently. Very differently. Throughout college, my drinking was tempered by the fact that I didn't have much money. That all changed when I got a desk job. The shackles of financial destitution were gone. Every time I went out I hit it hard. Really hard.

On one occasion, I turned up for a public work event still plastered from the night before. My boss noticed but said nothing. My breath stank of booze and I was so dehydrated and sick I could only manage to sip a bottle of water through the whole day.

The last big blowout was at birthday party in a friend of a friend's flat. I barely knew the girl or her friends so I got blind drunk in the kitchen. One of my crew had to sacrifice the rest of his night by driving me home.

I look back on this time, not with regret, but with thankfulness of what it taught me. I also see Divine protection from the darkest times and most dangerous nights. You regularly hear of (mostly young) men who have a heavy night and die after falling asleep outside or drowning in a lake after an ill-thought out midnight swim. I could have easily been one of them.

### Going Sober Was my Only Option

I used to think that having a drinking problem meant living in squalor while drinking high strength cider from a blue plastic bottle. Or doing an

'Alice Cooper' (who reportedly drank a bottle of whiskey for breakfast at the height of his alcoholism). But now I'm convinced of this: You don't need to be an alcoholic to have a dysfunctional relationship with alcohol. In all my time of heavy drinking, I wasn't an addict. But I did drink for the wrong reasons.

I drank to lose control and sometimes to hurt myself. I didn't enjoy drinking per se but I did like the buzz of being less accountable for my actions and more unpredictable. I liked to be the guy who could drink the most and still stay upright. The flipside is that I hated the person I became when I was drunk. It was as if all of my negative character traits were amplified to intolerable levels.

Looking back, I can see how I'd got into a negative habit loop of FOMO (Fear of Missing Out), self-destructiveness, and release through a lack of self-respect. Eventually an older friend sat me down and told me that I was out of control. I decided there and then to go sober. When I sat on that sofa talking to my friend, I had no option but to give it up. It had to be all or nothing. At least until I could control my drinking – where it was positive and not destructive. I went home and emptied the wine and vodka I kept in the house down the sink. At the time, I felt nothing – no catharsis, no regret. Just numb.

A few weeks later some of my work colleagues were going out to a bar. When I told them I'd given up drinking they laughed. I was the life and soul of the party – I had to be joking, right?

But it wasn't enough for me to be 'that guy who doesn't drink'. I also withdrew myself from situations where alcohol was being consumed: I didn't go to bars or clubs. On my wedding day, I drank coffee and diet coke. It was the only way I could guarantee that I wouldn't slip up. I had been engaged in a gradual but definite spiral to a place that, ultimately, I didn't want to go.

## It's Harder to Gain Weight When You Don't Drink

If you drink heavily, you'll know about one of the main side effects: weight gain. As a student, I would drink to excess and then pig out on takeaway foods, pizza and bar snacks. Then the following day I would be so hungover that I'd sleep until noon before I hit an all-day breakfast with a can full sugar soft drink. As a result, my weight would fluctuate like mad. At University I was active, playing sports and walking everywhere. But when I started working I was sitting down for most of the day and had a car. My waist size ballooned. Exercise was out of the question: I could barely run to the end of the street! But when I stopped drinking, I found that I didn't gain weight as easily. I didn't have hangovers anymore either (duh) so Saturday mornings could be spent walking to the shops or going for a run. Later, when I took up martial arts, I'd be fresh all the time while guys I trained with would be slower even if it had been a couple of days since they'd last had a drink.

At the time I gave up drinking, it felt like a HUGE deal. It was going to have a potentially massive impact on my lifestyle. How would I cope? At first it felt like I was giving something up – something of value to me. But in reality, I wasn't really losing, I was gaining. I achieved so much in the three years that I was sober that I don't regret giving up the booze. Not for one moment. But the main upshot was that I broke the self-destructive habit loop of drinking to excess on a regular basis and doing it for damaging reasons (a habit loop is when you are trapped in a vicious cycle of 'cue, routine, reward' - more on this later). Giving up drinking was a true turning point in my life. Sometimes giving something up allows you to gain so much more.

## What About Now?: My Journey From Drinking to the Present

Now it's nine years since I stopped drinking. But I was only completely dry for 3 years. Since then I've been able to enjoy alcohol in a positive and constructive way. I stopped drinking because it was something I couldn't control. But having that break from it changed everything to the point where I can control how I drink. I don't do it to mess myself up or to lose control. I do it socially, with friends or family and get pleasure from it. These days I rarely drink – the odd glass of wine here and there or a single malt on a Saturday night.

So why write this down? Because I know that there's every chance you've gone through or are going through something similar. Maybe it's with drink. But it might be with something else. My main regret with drinking is that no-one sat me down earlier and told me that I was being an idiot sooner. The first time it happened, I quit on the spot. If you are able to identify with these words, maybe it's time to quit. Suffering the ridicule and shame of your social grouping is a small price to pay for a better quality of life for you and the people around you. It will also make you stronger in the long run.

**The Problem of Pornography**

This next section first appeared on my blog in 2016. I started that post off with a disclaimer of sorts. When I sat down to write this book, I knew that there are wide range of Dads that are going to read it including close family and friends. So, here's a heads up: The remainder of this chapter is going to contain real talk, most of which is from my own experiences or from other Dads I know. If you think that you might be offended or unduly shocked by what you're going to read, do yourself a favour and skip to the next section. Otherwise, keep reading...

First off, I'm going to make some assumptions about you the reader:

- You're male
- You've engaged with pornography
- You don't believe it's been a positive experience

Maybe you don't fit these categories or you might even be a pornography advocate. If so keep reading - maybe I can convince you of my case.

When I write 'engaging in pornography' this is what I mean: viewing pornographic videos or images and masturbating at the same time, normally to climax. Most Dads my age have done it at some point or other. Some do it regularly. Others more occasionally – but then if you're a Dad my age, you already knew that didn't you?

Imagine you are back in 1997-98. This is long before the days of high speed broadband and pornography was more difficult to obtain. It existed as grainy jpegs on obscure sites, shaky VHS tapes and in the form of top shelf magazines with the front page covered. It took guts to walk into a porno shop and buy what you wanted. Most self-respecting men didn't or made do with the underwear section of the Next Directory.

These days, the availability and scale of porn is truly biblical. in 2014, the porn industry in the USA was estimated as being valued at $13 billion. To put that figure in context, the entire US iron and steel industry was worth $113 billion in the same year. Porn is worth more than 10% of the steel industry to Americans. One internet search and a few clicks will give you access to more pornography than you could view in an entire lifetime. But if the use of pornography is so prolific in Western Countries, can it really be such a problem for Dads?

**My Problem with Pornography**

I've always seen pornography as being negative. I was brought up in a traditional Christian home so it wasn't something that was spoken of in a positive light. But when I grew up and was old enough to make choices for myself, I knew deep down that what I was engaging in was negative, destructive and wasteful.

Added to that, I've never bought into the 'pornography is therapy' idea which goes along the lines of:

- Pornography is a normal part of male (and female) sexuality
- It can be enjoyed as part of a secure sexual relationship

- There are few negative effects as long as you're not addicted

But I could never crystallise these conclusions enough to take any positive form of action. I had read often of people suffering from pornography addiction. The actor Terry Crews (*The Expendables/Brooklyn 99*) is a well-known recovering addict. He admits that his use of pornography nearly destroyed him and his marriage. My own porn use never reached that level of engagement where it became a compulsive addiction though I can see how it might be for some men and Dads in particular.

There is also a popular argument that pornography encourages unrealistic expectations when translated into real life sexual experiences. Some feminists even claim that pornography usage causes rape fantasies and actual rape. Again, these arguments were never consistent with my own healthy and functioning sex life.

A third argument is this: That pornography is demeaning and to women and all (female) pornographic actors are somehow victims of a global abuse network. This would be easier to believe if the industry wasn't worth so much: Top female porn actors have a net worth in the tens of millions of dollars.

Does that mean that I don't believe there are *any* porn actors subject to abuse or coercion? No, obviously. But it's naive to suggest that the whole industry is one big conspiracy against women with thousands of unwilling and unpaid participants. That idea simply doesn't stack up with the undeniable presence of multi-millionaire porn actresses.

That's why I'm not convinced that the main problems with porn are:

- Widespread and sanctioned abuse and debasement of women
- Unrealistic expectations of real life sexual encounters
- Adverse effects on healthy marriages and partners

Why? Because these 'problems' focus on everyone except the user. The effects on the man engaging in pornography is discounted as being of secondary importance. After all he does it willingly and out of choice, doesn't he? Or does he...

If you are regularly engaging in pornography, the main person being affected by it (and the person who you should be most concerned with) is YOU. Y-O-U. No one else. You are the one who has to deal with whatever consequences there are from your actions. When I started to see my own engagement in pornography in this context, things began to change.

### The Science Bit: Pornography breeds Torpidity

Here's the (non imaginary) scene: You're finally alone in the house. Your wife has gone out and the kids are at a friend's house or upstairs asleep. You flick on the T.V. but there's nothing on. You look at your phone. The screen is blank. Your eye catches your laptop which looks like it's just finished charging. The doors are locked and the curtains closed. You flip the top and press the power button. Another evening alone.

What are the physiological effects from engagement with pornography? When you engage in porn (masturbate and eventually ejaculate) this triggers a series of physiological and hormonal effects in your body. Once you've finished, your body is in what scientists call the 'refractory period'. During this time, your body produces hormones in response to the simulated sexual experience. Two of these that I want to focus on are *Oxytocin* and *Prolactin*.

#### 1. Oxytocin

Oxytocin has a variety of functions in both men and women. For women, it has function during childbirth and in breast feeding. In men, it is released following sexual climax which produces a feeling of contentment, reduced anxiety and a feeling of calm and safeness. Scientists also believe oxytocin to be an important hormone for the inhibition of the brain regions associated with behavioural control and fear.

Oxytocin behaves like a drug following porn engagement making you feel chilled out and safe. This has an important function after intercourse - who wants to feel edgy afterwards? While important during intercourse it has very little benefit to you as you sit alone in your house while your wife is at her book club.

Plus, look at those physical effects. The release of oxytocin makes you:

- Feel content
- Less anxious
- Feel more calm and secure

These are all stupefying effects that bleed the energy out of your life and kill your motivation dead. Is that really what you want?

**2. Prolactin**

Like oxytocin, prolactin is a common hormone and is found in numerous organisms. In men, it is released following ejaculation and is responsible for the sense of sexual satisfaction you feel after sex. Simply, this hormone makes you feel the 'release' after climax. It contributes to the feeling of relaxation and is why you'll normally drift off to sleep after sex. Prolactin makes you sleepy.

That sounds great - almost like a natural sleeping pill. I mean, if pornography helps you sleep, it's not so bad is it? See for yourself: While prolactin is a naturally occurring hormone in relation to sexual intercourse, it also has some less desirable effects. For example, overproduction can lead to reduced testosterone and has been linked to erectile dysfunction and loss of libido (sex drive).

## Conclusions

When you engage in porn it's a big like being on very harmful drugs. Porn could be reducing your testosterone levels and is certainly contributing to you losing your edge. Porn is changing you from a lion to a sleepy, torpid little dormouse who has just woken up from hibernation.

## Porn Availability – A Global Conspiracy?

I'm going to make a little detour here so bear with me. Here's a thought experiment of mine: What if the widespread availability of pornography in Western countries was part of a wider conspiracy?

Here are the facts:

- Pornography is celebrated as 'therapy' or 'art'
- Porn usage and availability in Western countries is at record levels
- Pornography is generally legal and unregulated in Western Europe, North and South America
- There is a sustained and persistent attack on the role of men within society including a portrayal of male identity and energy as something toxic
- There are very real physiological effects on men who engage in pornography that include changing from lions to sleepy little kittens.

Coincidence? Maybe, but I don't believe in coincidences. So, what if the proliferation of pornography was permitted as a tool of governments to keep men in check. To keep us happy, stupid and sleepy?

A man who is slow and sleepy is a lot easier to control and manipulate. If you feel content and satisfied, you wouldn't object *too* much if you thought you were being taken advantage of, would you? Why is it that this drug-like-response is available to all when treatments to make men sharper and younger are tightly controlled?

But hey, you'd be mad to believe in all that conspiracy bull-crap, right?

## Addiction and the Habit Loop

Here's the thing: I'm not qualified to talk about addiction. I've no idea what the likes of Terry Crews and the thousands of other men who are searching 'pornography addiction' on Google every day are going through. But there has been a lot of research into habits and how they form. Charles Duhigg, author of *The Power of Habit: Why We Do What We Do and How to Change* is one of the leading writers on the subject. Habits form into a circular loop of Cue, Routine, Reward.

The negative habit of a Dad engaging in pornography would look like this:

**Cue**: You're alone in the house and have time to spare. You feel secure enough that you're not going to be discovered halfway through. This might be compounded with feelings of stress, anxiety or sexual frustration from a longer than normal period without sex.

**Routine**: You flip the laptop, click to your favourite porn site, find your favourite videos and away you go.

**Reward**: 15-35 minutes later you're done. The physiological feelings described earlier kick in although these are always tempered with a degree of guilt and annoyance that you couldn't find anything better to do with your time.

Duhigg's book gives good step by step suggestions to breaking habits so I'm not going to rehash his ideas although I am going to reveal my own experiences of success and eventual freedom from this habit. The key to breaking a habit is to break the loop. Once the cycle of habitual behaviour is broken, you'll find it much easier to avoid the destructive behaviour you've been trying to beat all these years.

## How to I Broke the Pornography Habit Loop

It will be no surprise that the 'sample' habit loop I described above is close to my own experiences. The cues were as follows:

- Stressed/anxious or sexually frustrated
- Alone/secure in the house
- Time enough to spare
- Nothing better to do

Breaking the habit loop and replacing the 'routine' that responds to the same cues changes my behaviour. The cues can be hard to change except maybe the last one. You normally *do* have something better to do. Here's how I've broken the habit loop: I write.

Writing has become my new habit. I might be writing a book (like I'm doing now) or a blog post or working on ideas, fixing my website or even doing some freelancing.

My evenings are filled with a productive activity that doesn't involve jerking off in the dark with a blue, hazy screen for company.

Think about your own porn usage. Can you identify the cues that lead to you engaging in pornography and change the routine? You don't have to write. It could be sometime as simple as walking the dog or making a cup of coffee when you feel the cues kicking in. A friend of mine took to smoking a cigarette whenever he felt the urge although it's probably better to replace porn with a habit that isn't going to give you cancer!

If you can break that habit loop in some way you absolutely can break the pornography habit until you reach a point like me when you can't even remember the last time you engaged in porn.

## Giving Up Porn: Harness Your Energy Through Sexual Transmutation

Sexual transmutation of energy sounds like something you'd find in a Marvel comic book. But it's actually a pretty simple concept (and has been around for a while). Napoleon Hill wrote extensively on the subject in his seminal work '*Think and Grow Rich*'. Here's the theory: If you could harness your sexual energy and divert a proportion of it into another activity, you have the potential to be unstoppable.

Think back to your 20's – if you had used some of that raw sexual energy you had as a young man to build a business, property empire or learn Cantonese, where would you be now? A self-made real estate investor in Beijing?

Through breaking the habit loop and transferring that energy into my writing, I've written tens of thousands of words and reached thousands of people. I've been able to write this book - something I'd never have thought possible. You only get so much energy in one lifetime. It's a finite resource. Now think about the time and energy you've spent engaging in pornography. It's been a waste, hasn't it?

## A Future without A Pornography Habit

This is your chance here and now to carve a future without a pornography habit. If that's the decision you make, do you think you'll ever regret it? Probably not. Why not join me and thousands of other fathers in resolving to live a porn free life.

In summary:

1. Pornography is a problem – not because it's demeaning to women, wrecks relationships or can be addictive for some but because of the negative effects it has on you – the user.
2. The body responds to simulated ejaculation (following porn usage) in a negative and destructive way. The last thing you want to be is slow, sleepy and testosterone deprived.

3. The reluctance to regulate pornography in any meaningful way by Western governments while other less destructive activities and products are banned or tightly controlled is highly suspicious.
4. My porn habit fitted snugly into the widely recognised MIT research communicated by Charles Duhigg on habit loops involving cue, routine and reward.
5. This habit loop has been broken through transmutation of that energy into a more productive activity – my writing.

Isn't it time you dreamed of a porn free life? Once you live it you'll never look back.

**Conclusion: Final Thoughts on Spirituality and Self Control**

It would be great if being religious or self-controlled and disciplined instantly solved all of your problems and allowed you to live a carefree life. But it doesn't. Just because you beat your habit of porn usage or self-destructive drinking doesn't mean you'll be free from other habits and problems like secret eating, body dysmorphia or anxiety. But if you're putting in the work every day to better yourself you will find it becomes easier to break habits and live a more positive and productive life - and pass these good habits on to your kids when you're older.

My Christian faith has become a foundation on which the rest of my life depends. I have an unbreakable relationship with Jesus Christ who loved me so much that he'd willingly be tortured and die in my place. I can't ever pay that back but I can live my life as if I'd like to.

If religion motivates and drives you, then you know what I mean. If you consider yourself to be a-religious or atheistic, examine the reasons for this. Are you making an informed decision? If so then I'm not going to persuade you otherwise. But if you have doubts in what you believe in, pull at these doubts and examine them. Part of a father's mission is to be a lifelong explorer - it may not change your mind but it might just enrich your life.

References:

http://www.mayoclinic.org/diseases-conditions/prolactinoma/basics/definition/con-20028094

## Pillar 4: The Power of Knowledge

*"Knowledge is knowing* that a *tomato is a fruit. Wisdom is not putting* it in a *fruit salad*" - Miles Knighton

What do we understand by the word 'knowledge'? And what place does knowledge have in a father's mission? You might imagine a library when you think of 'knowledge' but does a library contain knowledge? Aren't books just pages with words in them? Those words only become knowledge when you allow the concepts to enter into and be applied to your thinking.

As a younger man, I studied applied theology. It was a course that contained a deep vein of practical application. The concept was simple: A theoretical subject like religion has no practical application if it remains confined to the pages of a book.

Over time my reading habits have changed. I used to read junk fiction and magazines until I realised that his was a big waste of time, not to mention money. Gradually I started to claw my reading habits back until I was reading only non-fiction biographies and business books. That was pretty hardcore and couldn't last. That phase has since passed and I try to mix up my reading with a range of fiction and nonfiction.

So what the heck is this part of the book all about? It's about several things and although I've called it Wisdom and Knowledge, it could have other titles like 'Books and Comprehension', 'Personal Development' or something equally dry. But before we go deeper into books and knowledge, what do we understand the word 'knowledge' to mean?

If you break knowledge down into its constituent parts you're left with the following: Learning, Understanding and Applying. Without these three aspects of knowledge working in tandem together your knowledge would be incomplete. All of these parts must work together and complement each other. You could say it's the holy trinity of knowledge.

## Learning

Since the day we first opened our eyes we've been learning. As a young child, you learned at an incredible rate. Studies have even shown that young babies can learn responses to stimuli while they sleep! Now that's impressive. Some experts believe that's why children sleep so much - because their brains are being filled with information and lessons all day long as they strive to make sense of the world around them.

But you'd have to admit that your learning slows down as you relax into the patterns of adulthood. Think about it: when was the last time you learned a new skill or subject. Sure, there are a few people who learn languages or musical instruments later in life but for the most part, our skills and knowledge acquisition goes waaaay down the older we get.

How do we redress this imbalance? Is it time you took control of your own learning and directed it towards something productive and enduring? If you put down the remote, stopped watching Netflix in the evenings and taught yourself a new skill (or three) would you be more or less likely to live a happier and more fulfilled life?

## Understanding

What good is knowledge without comprehension? If you read and learn something, anything, but don't understand what you've learned, have you really gained anything? Living in Uganda, I witnessed the teaching style of a rural school. Classes contained over 100 pupils learning 'by rote'.

The idea with learning by rote is that if you repeat something for long enough you'll remember it. This kind of teaching is used for simple things like your times table or Latin verb endings. But when it comes to your own personal studying and learning, repetitive brain bashing won't cut it. After all, time is a precious commodity and you don't have much to spare. Any time you spend learning must be time well spent. So, it's imperative that learning is accompanied by understanding.

**Applying**

The third part of my holy trinity of knowledge is application. As with my theology diploma, the real value of knowledge is in the application. The Bible speaks about someone who doesn't apply knowledge as being like a man who sees his reflection in the mirror and then instantly forgets what he looks like. You can read all the informative and interesting books you like and learn all you can about a range of topics but if you are unable (or unwilling) to apply them to your life, have you not wasted your time. Some people would call this 'mental masturbation' - where you stimulate the mind for no gain whatsoever.

The alternative is to be mindful when you are going out of your way to learn new things. Ask yourself these questions as you learn:

- What am I reading/learning?
- What do I agree with or disagree with?
- How can I apply or use this information in my day to day life?
- What am I going to do differently today having learned this?

If you practise this discipline as you learn and read, you'll gain true knowledge from your own time of study and learning instead of reading words that retain no meaning for you in the longer term.

**The Value of Knowledge for Modern Fatherhood**

I've devoted a large proportion of my life to making myself a better person - father, husband, son and employee. A significant part of that journey has been through reading and personal study. I'm in a good position to write this book because of what I've learned through my personal experience *and* the experiences of others - those that I've read about in books or online.

Sure, you can learn by watching the Discovery Channel or the news (up to a point!) but this type of learning by osmosis is deeply inefficient. Think about watching a news channel like Bloomberg to learn about business. At least 25% of your time is spent watching ads for the latest Forex trading platform while another 10% is wasted by talking heads that don't know any more than you do - if they were so hot on stock tips, would they be getting paid to give their thoughts on TV?

It's only by reading that you can gain a true and deep understanding of a subject. Even audiobooks are flawed in this respect. I find myself 'tuning' in and out of a narrated book. It's useful to soak up a commute but are you getting the same benefit as reading the words on a page or screen?

Knowledge increases your personal value. The more you know and understand, the more value you can bring to other people's lives - including your kids. A father's mission must include the desire and discipline of acquiring and applying knowledge.

Most people know not to take life advice from a teenager - they haven't lived long enough to acquire the knowledge that a man in his forties has. Knowledge can be a transferrable attribute - if you understand more about business and sales are you more or less likely to be good at managing and gaining new clients at your place of work?

**Where to Read**

Where is the best place to read? You can pretty much read anywhere you like. I've got my own preferences: a nice comfy arm chair, bed or on a train. But you might have different places - the local library, your office before work or in the car while you wait for your daughter to finish her ballet/Jiu jitsu/art class.

It doesn't really matter where you read as long as it's a place where you'll have minimal distractions. What do I mean by that? For me it means no background noise or people talking to you. Thankfully British people don't talk to strangers so public transport are quiet places in general. I can't read if there is a TV on in the room but the radio is fine as long it's classical music, otherwise I'll struggle to take in what I'm reading.

Bedtime is a good time to read. Reading before bed has been shown to be powerful stuff - some studies suggest that it can reduce your stress levels by up to 68%. Contrast this with getting your last social media fix before bed. Modern social media apps are designed to stimulate your senses. The feeds of apps like Twitter, SnapChat and Instagram behave like mini slot machines, triggering your senses and making you more alert. Reading has been shown to have the opposite effect.

### How to Gain Knowledge

Over this section of the book, we're going to take a deeper look into books. You clearly like reading as you 1) bought this one and 2) made it this far. So, I'll save the sermons on why books are amazing. You already value books which means I'm able to show you how you can get more out of reading and gaining the knowledge you need to be a better Dad and man in general.

We're going to look at how to build an awesome book collection and how to shoehorn in more reading time (that's the holy grail right there). We'll also look at the types of books to read and some tricks I've picked up along the way to maximise your reading time.

## *Chapter 1: How to Build an Awesome Book Collection*

There's something about books. I don't mean the digital ones you download on a whim from the Kindle store. I mean paperback, glossy cover, 'smell the newness' printed books. There is a physical connection between you and the book that you just don't get pushing the buttons or swiping the screen of an e-reader. If you're reading this in paperback, you know what I'm talking about. Owning physical, paper books also allows you to build up an impressive collection to display to anyone who visits and show your kids how much you love the written word.

But how do you start building an awesome book collection? It can be a daunting prospect if you don't really own many books and don't have anywhere to store them. Keep reading and I'll reveal everything. But first, we're going to take a trip back in time...

### My Childhood Love of Books Begins

My love of books started early on. Every week I would get a small amount of pocket money to spend how I liked. If I wanted a new toy or a comic I would use my allowance or save up until I had enough. When it came to buying books, it was a different game. If I saw a book I wanted, my parents would get it for me - as long as it wasn't banal or a waste of money.

This grant system for book buying taught me a valuable lesson: my parents valued books and reading to the point that they would spend the little money they had to help me learn and read more books. It also meant that I didn't resent buying books - my pocket money was ring fenced for Lego toys or more 'Ammo King' ammunition for my cap-pistol.

As I grew older my love of books continued and developed too. When I was eight years old my teacher commented on how I was able to enter 'my own little world' when reading a good book. Later as an early teen I was often shunned or bullied by my peers and would retreat into a good book once my homework and study was done.

When I lived in rural Uganda, there wasn't much to do on evenings and weekends other than read and write. So, I did a lot of both. It was during that time that I read many classics and books on theology and spirituality and reading the Bible through for the first time.

In the last few years, something changed. I've gone from a book reader to a book collector. I love having a bookshelf in my home to display to myself and my children the value that I have placed on books, both for learning and entertainment.

Recently I stopped reading magazines and other 'junk' literature and put that time into reading more books. Most magazines exist to sell you products via advertising. Fitness magazines are one of the worst offenders for this with over half the pages containing product ads or endorsements. So, I stopped buying them. Now I've been consistently buying both paper and electronic books until I'm at the stage where I need more shelf space to accommodate all the titles I own.

But an awesome book collection has to start somewhere. And if you're struggling to know where that somewhere is, this chapter is going to be of immense use. Even if you've got a few books and shelves, I'm going to give you tools and knowledge to make it go from 'OK' to 'freaking awesome'.

**Step 1: Get a Good Bookcase**

When was the last time you went to someone's house and they had a bulging bookcase full of all kinds of titles? For me, it's a while although I do have some friends and family members who share my love of literature and learning. The truth is that most people don't own many books and recent studies have suggested that 60% of people in the UK don't read a single book in any one year.

If you're going to build an awesome book collection, you'll need somewhere to store them. Boxes don't really cut it for me. What you need is a proper book shelf or even better, a book case. A few decades ago book cases were hard to get. But thankfully we now live in the world of mass produced flat pack Swedish furniture where a good case can be bought for under £100. It's worth investing in a good bit of useful furniture like a book case.

Hopefully you'll always love books and they can be very decorative in a living space. A case with shelves that can be set at different heights is especially useful - that way you can store a range of titles and genre from reference books to airport paperback novels.

**Step 2: Buy Some Books**

Where is the best place to buy books? If you want to you can buy new releases from Amazon or the high street but this can become expensive if you are buying new all the time. The truth is there are some great deals to be made if you know where to look or have the patience.

I used to buy a lot of books in charity or second-hand shops. More recently I've stopped doing this as many of these stores aren't offering real savings and it can be time consuming to find something you'd like to read. It can take your hours to browse through all the junk and crime fiction just to find a title you'd actually like to read.

Thankfully there are tools that make your life easier. The ones I use the most are the Amazon Wishlist and Recommendations to find books that I'd like to read. Amazon is the biggest retailer of new books - you knew that right? But did you also know it's the biggest retailer of *second hand books?* I didn't think so. Most books that are still in print (and a few that are out) can be picked up for as little as a penny (plus postage). If I sound like a convert it's because I am. I've lost count of the good deals I've got on difficult-to-find or otherwise extortionately priced books by buying second hand.

If you see or hear of a book you'd like, add it to your Amazon wishlist (the Amazon app is good for doing this on the go), then Amazon will tailor recommendations based on your list and any previous purchases to build up a picture of the kind of things you like to read. It's like a big reading circle of life but instead of the lions eating the gazelles, you get to eat books. Well metaphorically at least.

If you also read a lot of Kindle (more on this later) you can 'highlight' books that get mentioned or cited in the volume you're reading and then look for it later. These highlights are stored in your device allowing you to add them to your Amazon Wishlist at a later date.

**Step 3: Scam some Free Books**

I'm Scottish. And so naturally I love getting things for free and books are no exception. But where can you pick up books for free? You could look in skips or dumpsters or on your local Freecycle or Craigslist message board for 'Free to a Good Home' listings. However, with this approach you run the risk of acquiring boxes of cheap paperbacks with almost nothing useful to read.

If your parents have good taste in books (as mine do) then you're in luck. You could offer to re-home some of their books for free. They get rid of some clutter and you get free books. Now that's what I call a win-win. You could also do a swap with a book loving friend - are there any titles that you're done with and would like to trade? You could even set up a book-swap-meet and raise money for a men's charity in the process.

**Step 4: Organise Your Collection**

One of my pet hates is a poorly organised bookshelf. I've even been in book stores where the titles weren't even arranged alphabetically by author. Or even genre. I KNOW!!! There's no excuse for having a disorganised book collection. It will take you around an hour to organise your books, depending on how many you have (I'm probably at around

200). Keeping your shelves organised, whether that's alphabetised, by genre or even colour of the cover, will help you find a book or put away one you've recently finished. Numerous studies have shown that mess increases stress levels and especially in women. So even if you're not organising your books for yourself, you could be doing it for the benefit and sanity of your other half.

**Can you Afford Not to Have a Book Collection?**

So, you love books and want to increase your knowledge? Prove it. The only way you can really walk that walk is by acquiring books and (of course) reading them. It makes sense to build a book collection - it's like a record of your journey of knowledge for posterity and for your kids.

One of my greatest hopes is that many of my books will one day become my children's and that they will derive the same amount of pleasure that I have in reading them. If you share in that vision, start collecting today.

We truly are a privileged generation. We have such a wide access to books, literature and information that our forebears could barely even dream about. You can log onto Amazon and buy nearly any title of any book you want, often at a great price. Don't squander this opportunity you've been given - for the sake of those who have gone before you and for your family's future.

## *Chapter 2: How to Read More Even if You Have Young Kids*

Finding time to read more can be a real challenge. Add young children into the mix and it can be near impossible. So how do you manage your time better so that you can still have time with your kids and time to read and absorb knowledge.

There needs to be a balance doesn't there? You can't shut yourself away in a room with a book while your kids pound on the door asking you to help them do homework/rescue the cat/build the most awesome Hot Wheels track ever seen. How do I know this? I've tried.

So, you're going to need to be a bit more inventive when it comes to finding time and space to read. By the time you've worked out, killed it at your day job and generally been an awesome Dad there aren't many hours left in the day to sit with a book or your Kindle. So how do you manage to get time to read free from the distraction of young children?

### Get Up Early to Maximise Your Time

Let's face it: Long lies are done. And I mean they're over, probably for ever. By the time your kids have the ability to sleep in and *not* wake you at 6am because their teddy fell down the side of the bed and they can't reach him/her, you'll have lost the ability to snooze completely. Which is fine by me. I spent some of my prime years lying uselessly in bed.

I'm making up for lost time.

Mornings are when I do my best work. I'm sharper, more focused and generally less hyped up on caffeine. I also take time to read. I'll purposely get up an hour before everyone else so I can prepare breakfast and get in a good 20-30 minutes of reading while I eat. A Kindle is great for mealtime reading as there are no pages to turn and therefore no porridge or egg yolk to smear across the pages of your copy of *Tools of Titans*.

If you do this, it's worth choosing your reading material carefully. If you need to run to a tight schedule in the mornings (who doesn't?) then getting caught up in a fiction thriller probably isn't a good idea. Instead I prefer non-fiction books on business or writing as these are considerably easier to dip in and out of than fiction or philosophy.

**Read More by Using Work Breaks Productively**

If you work in an office, you should be taking regular screen breaks. A screen break is a 2-5-minute break away from your computer screen. You could walk around, get a coffee, take a leak or water your plants. It's a good excuse rest your eyes from the all-pervasive blue light you've been subjected to since the age of 21 (or younger). You could also read a few pages of a book. It takes an average reader around 3-5 minutes to read one page. Add that up over several breaks a day, 5 days a week and you'll be making real reading progress.

I would also advise taking a lunch break. Go somewhere where you won't be distracted and read. Even if it's for 20 minutes while you drink your 5th coffee, that's better than nothing. If you're heading to a meeting, allow for extra time for delays. If you arrive early, read for a few minutes. You'll feel calmer when your meeting starts.

If you travel with work, always take plenty to read. I do some of my best reading when I'm away from home. I can easily read two whole books while travelling overnight with work. Plan in advance what books you want to take with you.

**Pack a Book in the John**

Where's the one place you can get total peace for a few minutes? The Can. You go in there, bolt the door and you're alone. Finally. But instead of surfing your Amazon Wishlist, take a book in there with you. Yes, it might take you a while to read Homer's *The Iliad* but it will take you a whole lot longer if you don't start.

I like to have something a little humorous in the 'Throne Room' - I recently planted a book in there that covered the sustainable treatment of sewage which is very relevant for that specific activity. It was also an excellent read for a sustainability and self-sufficiency geek like me.

## Go to Bed Earlier. And Read

When was the last time there was something good on TV after 10pm? Even the news is poorly produced – more features and opinions than current events. Could you be using that time better? If you'd normally hit the hay at 10.30, give yourself an extra half hour to read. Reading before bed could even help your sleep better: Better sleep is important if you're expecting night time feeds, nappy changes or general '*Daddy, I had a nightmare.*' interruptions.

Something 'light' is probably best at this time of night. I'd leave the post-apocalyptic thrillers or history of cold war Poland for another time of day. A bit of light fiction or biography is probably a better choice if you're looking to de-stress.

If you flop into bed at eleven o'clock at night exhausted, you could be wasting valuable reading time. If you went to bed 30 minutes earlier and managed to read for 20 minutes per day, that works out at an extra 121 hours of reading per year. That's long enough to read Tolstoy's *War and Peace* through twice. These small moments of snatched reading time really add up - even a few pages per night is going to significantly increase the number of books you read over the course of a year.

## Audiobooks Transform a Long Commute

For the hard working, hard reading Dad you are there is a secret weapon: the audiobook. An audio books can transform your commute (driving or otherwise) into a journey of learning and discovery. Now that the digital age is here, you don't even need to fumble around with CDs at traffic lights either. Just a few taps on your phone and you've got access to thousands of titles.

One of my best investments was a subscription to Audible - that's the Amazon audiobook service. You get 1 credit each month to buy an audiobook of your choice. I've listened to over twenty titles over the course of a year and particularly enjoy biography and science books.
One question I've been asked regularly is this: How much to you take in while you're driving? The truth is 'it depends'. Firstly, it depends on how good and engaging the book is. Some of the books I've listened to have been pretty dull and difficult to get through.

Taking that into consideration, I'd say around 20-30 per cent of a book if I'm really concentrating. Remember what we said at the start of this section: knowledge comes from learning, understanding and application. Of what I learn, I probably understand around half of the concepts. So, 10-15 per cent reading comprehension and retention.

Which is pretty poor isn't it? Or is it. Some people estimate that you retain about 10 percent of a book's information when you *read* it. So, when you listen to a recording, it's about the same. Remember: retaining 10 percent of a book's information is infinitely more than if you didn't read it in the first place.

There really is no excuse for not reading more. Sure, you might have to snatch a few moments here and there while you take care of your fatherly duties. But you owe it to yourself to read more and especially more books.

I've successfully read dozens of titles by snatching a few pages whenever I get the chance. You'll find that delays or traffic jams are a lot more bearable if you spend the time reading. Getting to bed early takes discipline but reading books and acquiring knowledge is it's own reward and will lead you down the path of being a better man and father.

**Summary: Every Dad Can Read More**

If you want knowledge you're going to have to read. Watching Discovery Channel repeats is entertaining but what are you really learning? Books provide more detail and insight that you can reasonably get from television and films.

I guarantee you can read more than you are right now. I know you *can* read. I know that because you got to Pillar four out of six! Most men just read the first few pages of a book and give up. But there are real ways you can read more right now. Today.

That might mean switching off your phone or getting up/going to bed a little earlier. Maybe you need to install an audiobook app on your phone or turn a few pages at lunch time. Small increments of reading time add up over the course of a year and a lifetime. To borrow a phrase from Napoleon the Great, the best time to start reading more is ten years ago. The next best time is today.

Yes, you could read anything but if you want more knowledge - learning and applying - non-fiction books should be your priority. If you're unsure what subject to read, pick one that interests you and take it from there. Maybe you're into sports biographies or adventure books. Or you could prefer books on tech start-ups. Whatever you're into - read about it then move onto another subject. Read with an open mind - you're not going to agree with everything you see. But if you approach with an open mind you might just have your views challenged, if not changed.

I can't imagine a life without books. And it's been a pleasure to write one. I hope you're enjoying it as much as I've enjoyed writing it for you.

**Action:** Make a deal with yourself to read an extra 20 minutes per day. When is entirely up to you. And make sure it's something worthwhile - catalogues and magazines don't count.

## Pillar 5: The Power of the Outdoors

If you've ever spent any time in the outdoors, you know that it has immense power. Step into a forest, mountain or hillside and you'll be struck by the incredible scale and size of the world. A night sky allows you to visualise a near infinite landscape of stars, planets and galaxies.

It's no surprise that you should feel a strong connection with the outdoors. Until recently you'd have spent much more time there. It's only in our post-industrial modern times that we enjoy a mainly sedentary, indoor lifestyle.

But is 'enjoy' the right word? Despite all our home comforts; central heating, on demand food and entertainment, is something missing? And what will this ultimately mean for the next generation?

As a father with a vision of your kid's future, you want them to experience and learn to value everything this great world has to offer. That should include a healthy relationship with the outdoors. I grew up playing in woods, climbing mountains and wading through rivers. As a school boy, I'd work in my small garden growing vegetables in my spare time. Mud and dirt were my friends and the great wide-open spaces of the Scottish mountains were my playground.

The outdoors has power because through that environment you are able to channel your male energy (what others call masculinity) and that of your sons into something positive and worthwhile. Whether that's scaling a peak, paddling a rapid, hunting a deer or just walking through the park, you have the opportunity and the tools to commune with your environment on a deeper level than most people will ever experience. You have the opportunity to become completely unplugged from the 'Matrix' of the internet, social media and all the demands that this technology puts on your life.

Now that's real power.

But what if you've become detached from the outdoors? You used to go to the country or your local park all the time but recently, you're just not feeling it. It's too easy to stay inside on a cold spring afternoon and watch the game or go watch a movie. But are you creating the kinds of memories, lessons and experiences you want for you and your children? If not, what can you do. How can you rediscover your love of the outdoors and see it all again as something fresh, new and exciting?

That's what this pillar is about - rediscovering that love of the outdoors. Sure, there will be days when it's wet, cold and windy and you don't want to leave the house. But often those are the days that shape your character the most.

We're going to start by following in the footsteps of my own father - an intrepid mountaineer in his own right. He climbed many a peak, often alone. We'll also look at outdoor play and how you can get more out of playing outside with your kids (hint: sometimes leaving them alone works best). After that, we'll head to the vegetable patch to learn about how we've become disconnected from where our food comes from. Is it too late to press 'reset' on this? Hopefully not.

***Chapter 1: Mountains, Memories and my Father***

I've climbed mountains since before I can remember. Even before I could walk, I was hoisted up various hills and peaks in a 1980's baby carrier. It was made of a metal frame and brown canvas and probably weighed a ton, especially with a chunky monkey like me in the back.

It was only natural that I would grow up walking and hiking in some of the UK's most impressive landscapes. For a brief time, I hated it – probably when I was between 7 and 10. It was hard to keep up with everyone and hiking boots for kids weren't what they are now. I used to have to take three or four steps for every one of my parents' and my short legs were a big disadvantage when it came to covering ground quickly. I'd often lag behind, calves burning from the initial exertion of the first ascent up the mountainside.

But when I reached my teens something changed. I started to feel an incredible spiritual connection with the rugged landscapes, cliffs and valleys. It was around this time I was learning geography at high school and how the process of glaciation had forced its will against the rock over millennia. I felt like I could see the surrounding landscape being formed in my mind's eye.

When I walked, it was as if the hills and valleys swallowed me up only to spit me out when I reached civilisation (or my parents' car) on the other side.

When I was 14, I was allowed to walk some of the Pennine way (in England) with my sister. We got lost and wandered into a deep bog. I was terrified. A half-rotted sheep was floating in the thick mud, grinning as if to say, 'join me….'. Eventually a helpful passer-by pointed us in the direction of the village we were staying. Lying awake that night I felt panicky but excited. What if we'd fallen into the bog and drowned? What if the nice man hadn't pointed out that our map was upside down. Would we still be out in the moor, struggling through stream and swamp?

Later on, into my teens I started to do more adventurous walks with my family and when I was 20 I started to do my own climbs in the Scottish Cairngorms. On one occasion, I walked solo along the Jock's Road - a mountain pass between two valleys (or glens). It was 15 miles from end to end and my parents agreed to pick me up at the other side. I eventually reached the other side footsore but elated. I had walked further that I'd imagined possible and climbed two peaks on the way. The April sun was setting as I fell asleep in the back of my father's Subaru, a smile on my face.

**My Father and his Mountaineering Legacy**

My Dad, an only child, married late. While my mum always had plenty of stories of her childhood and youth, my father had few. His life before he was married was an enigma to me growing up. I knew he'd been in the military and had done a lot of walking before he was married (he actually proposed to my mum on a hike). But there were 47 long years before I came along. What had he been doing in all that time? My own father, while a loving and wise man was a mystery to me.

Soon before my solo climb, my father gave me a quick map reading lesson and handed me a book titled 'Munro's Tables'. A 'Munro' is a Scottish mountain over 3000 feet tall. There are around 282 of these peaks with varying degrees of difficulty. Sir Hugh Munro was the first person to compile the list and his tables have stood the test of time with only a few revisions.

My father's copy of Munro's Tables is now one of my most treasured possessions. In it contains details of every climb he made in the years he lived in Scotland. Every high point is recorded with the date and who he did it with. Some are in winter and some are alone. As I thumbed the pages of that red leather-bound book, I finally understood. This was his story, his memories.

As a boy growing up, I was discouraged and disappointed that I wasn't part of this story. As my father aged to the point that he couldn't keep up with me, I longed to travel back in time to walk these epic mountain routes with him. But as I started to record the dates that I'd reached the same peaks, I finally began to understand the connection. I understood that our stories are interlinked. There might be almost 50 years separating them but his book and his enthusiasm for the mountains means we have a deeper connection than I could have ever hoped or wished for.

Now when I head to the hills that sense of spiritual awe remains but there is something else: I'm walking in the footsteps of my Dad. It's the closest we'll get to walking these routes together.

### Mountains, Me and My Son

My Dad is in his eighties now and following a stroke, his hill walking days are well and truly over. But the baton passes to me. It's my turn to explore these sacred places with my son. I don't plan on pushing him into doing anything he doesn't want to but at the same time I hope that he will grow up understanding the value that these places have for me and for his own heritage.

If you've been inspired to start hiking more with your kids, remember to take it easy with them. It's supposed to be an enjoyable experience. They'll grow up resenting the hills and you if you force them into it. Instead, make it fun and keep your hikes age appropriate. As they grow, you can escalate the difficulty and length up.

### Find your Mountain

Mountains are great metaphors in life for lots of things. I've been in the mountains at some of my lowest and highest points in life. Living in Uganda I used to retreat regularly to the mountains for prayer and meditation. It was an antidote to the stress of living in an alien and often hostile environment. Later as a recruit in the British army Reserve, my training regularly took place in the mountains and hills of Scotland. There was precious little time to enjoy the scenery while carrying over 100 pounds of ammunition and equipment over miles of rough track and terrain.

Mountains present a powerful metaphor for life. Mediocrity and passiveness says 'Don't climb the mountain, it will be too hard. Do it when you have more time.' Passion, perseverance and a sense of challenge says: 'I'll climb the mountain and I'll climb it today because it exists.'

## Final Thoughts

It's no wonder we feel deep connections with our landscape and the hills. Our ancestors would have known these places well: where's the best spot to fish, hunt and swim. To a certain extent we've lost that connection with our environment.

That's why it's important for those of us who still feel connected to pass that on to the next generation – so that they might know and understand their heritage and grow to respect this planet that we call home. When I reach the top of a mountain, I like to stand with my arms outstretched. I feel a part of the landscape, not a conqueror but a participant in something beautiful and massive.

### ***Chapter 2: How to Get More From Outdoor Play***

If you love and value the outdoors, it's only right that you'd want to pass that onto your kids. Studies have shown that children who have access to the outdoors do better at school, are healthier (duh) and have better relationships. But there's a problem.

A recent study reported in the London Telegraph showed that kids play outside for an average of 30 minutes per day and one in five children don't play outdoors at all. The idea that a child could grow up having never played outside is now a very real possibility.

How do you foster a love of the outdoors in your kids? If you're like me it can feel like an uphill struggle. They'd much rather be warm and dry in the house enjoying some 'screen-time'. But we know better than to let them indulge in this in perpetuity. Instead we know and value the outdoors and all it has to offer. If you're serious about your children's development, outdoor play has to be a central activity.

I love the outdoors. I can't remember a time in my life when I didn't love being outside. As a child, I'd play out in the garden – rain, sun, snow – all weathers were suitable. In school gym class, I used to prefer playing football and doing athletics in the rain. It felt more grown up to be allowed to get soaked and muddy while under adult supervision.

Now my kids are growing up, we get outside whenever we can. Where? We're not fussy: The park, garden, woods or even mountains. However, outdoor play can be a challenge. Once you include variables such as weather, rough ground and wild animals (ever met a Glasgow grey squirrel?) it can become a struggle. Especially with young children in tow.

It would be great if there were ways to enhance and improve your outdoor play with your kids. And there are. You don't need much preparation or resources. But you will need to be resourceful and let go of your inhibitions a little. So how can you make sure you get the most out of the outdoors and have a blast at the same time.

**Getting More out of Outdoor Play: Have a Plan**

I have to admit I'm not really a planning type. I like to try stuff and see what happens. Sometimes this is useful and productive. Other times – not so much. Outdoor play is definitely an activity that can benefit from having some sort of plan. I'm not talking about a lesson plan – it's not meant to be school. But it's helpful to have some kind of idea what you want to do – especially if you're going to be leading the play (not always necessary – keep reading to find out more).

Here are some ideas:

1. Do some light, age appropriate bushcraft or survival skills. When I say, 'age appropriate', I mean knife skills or fire lighting might not be suitable for under threes. But things like shelter building are. See if there are bushcraft classes in your area - Father/Son bushcraft lessons are popular so you'll need to book fast or get on that waiting list.
2. Build shelters and houses in the woods out of logs and branches. This can be done by kids from a young age. When my kids were two and four years old they had a blast building a house for the Gruffalo from the children's book of the same name.
3. Hide and Seek is an easy option for parks, woods and even your own back garden and young kids will love it. Toddlers will need help with hiding and counting though!
4. Buy a book of ideas. No this isn't cheating. An excellent book is *Commando Dad: Mission Adventure* by Neil Sinclair. It's packed with ideas and activities for outdoors and a few for a rainy day. You can follow it closely or use it as loose inspiration for your own outdoor play.

With these ideas and resources there's every opportunity to have a blast when playing outdoors. All you need is a little imagination and preparation. Your kids will grow up knowing and understanding the value of playing outside.

### Or you Could Not Have a Plan...

Here's a thought: Your kids don't always want you hovering over them like some kind of over protective Mummy-Eagle. Sometimes they want to play undisturbed by adults – to fight their own battles and settle disputes between each other without adult intervention or mediation. I know this comes as a blow – that you're surplus to requirements – but you need to accept it. And their mother does too. Whenever I'm in the park or out with the kids I see parents standing poised with their kids making sure NOTHING goes wrong. What they don't know is that I trained as a Playground Safety Inspector (yes that's a real thing). In my training, I was taught this shocking fact: Falling and pain are a part of active play and teach children about co-ordination, balance and perseverance. Who knew? The best thing about this approach is that you don't have to anything. Just sit and keep an ear out. Oh, and pack a first aid kit just in case.

### Incorporate Rough Play

I'm a big advocate for rough play for boys and girls. Rough-housing is an excellent way to build a strong bond with your kids, get active and burn off a few calories yourself. Imagine a world where rough play was banned. It would suck, wouldn't it? There would be a lot of messed up boys and girls who didn't know how to physically express themselves or their emotions. Physical play builds confidence and encourages self-expression and control. Emotional Intelligence shouldn't just be about sitting in a circle talking about 'Feel-Feels' (sorry, child psychology).

The outdoor environment is the perfect place to incorporate rough play. Think about it:

- No furniture to break
- No ornaments to smash
- No neighbours to think you're torturing spies in your front room (just me?)

Sometimes I'll just take a rugby ball to the park and mess around with my son. We're not really playing rugby – but it will be rough. The ball is secondary to the fun we'll be having. You could also try pretending to be a monster/zombie/bear and chasing your kids around the garden. Few Dads do this anymore which means you'll instantly be the cool dad who pretends to be a flesh-eating zombie.

**Adding Dimension to Outdoor Play: Use Props**

The use of props (sticks, balls, hoops or whatever you have lying around) can really add different dimensions to outdoor play sessions.

In the garden, a few buckets, balls and sticks can entertain kids for a long time. Remember: you might have to speak to the neighbours to ask for the 'Super High Bouncy Ball' back for the 50th time. And they already think you're weird with your obsessive lawn care regime and pipe smoking on summer evenings (again, this could just be me).

In the woods, props are all around. You could take a small folding spade and make some fortifications – but always check with the landowner before you dig in any woods. Take balls, kites, hoops, frisbees and boomerangs to the park. All of these add extra interest to your outdoor play. As a boy, I spent countless hours trying to get my boomerang to fly back to me before it finally got permanently lodged in the branches of an elm tree.

**Commit to Outdoor Play**

When I read about the lack of outdoor play some kids get, I actually feel sadness for them but mostly pity for their parents. They are missing out on A LOT of fun. I hope you've been inspired to play more outdoors and that this chapter has given you some great ideas and inspiration. Make it your mission to get your kids to play outdoors more and to enjoy the time they have with you. Remember, you don't need to hover over them all the time - sometimes they just want to be left to explore on my own. But it also makes sense to do a bit of preparation and have some ideas up your sleeve or even a few props! Any way you look at it, outdoor play is cheap, easy, great exercise and wears your kids out – what's not to love?

**Action:** Make your next weekend or day off devoted to outdoor play - it doesn't matter what as long as it's outside. Remember to have fun!

## *Chapter 3: How to Reconnect with the Land*

Let me start this chapter with a question: How connected are you to the land? I'm talking about the mucky, gritty stuff that you grow things in. Do you know how to grow and raise crops or trees or do you think that milk comes from cartons and potatoes from the vegetable aisle.

The truth is that our increasingly urbanised population is losing touch with the outdoors and the land in particular. My son recently asked me what factory the pork he was eating came from. More and more we've become detached from the land and in the way that it produces food for us to eat. But it wasn't always this way.

Rewind 200 years or so and you're in the days before the industrial revolution. You probably live in the country and you definitely don't have electricity, the internet or supermarkets. If you don't grow your own food, you'll die or at least be very poor and reduced to working for others just to eat.

In Europe, farming has been around for at least 4000 years and in other parts of the world for much longer. So, your ancestors were raising animals and crops, hunting and foraging for millennia before the recent few decades in which we've lost much of this knowledge. This isn't the case in other cultures however. Living in Uganda I came face to face with a primarily agrarian culture. Until 60 or 70 years ago, Ugandans were totally dependent on farming for survival. This has changed in urban areas but subsistence farming - where you farm primarily for your own use - is still commonplace in rural villages.

Even Ugandan city dwellers have small farms (called *shambas*) on the outskirts of their city or near their home villages. It's cheaper and easier to grow some crops than buy them in the supermarket or farmers markets. In the village where I lived in the north west of the country everyone grew their own crops and raised their own animals – even me. Farming in Uganda is a family affair with young children working alongside their parents. One farmer who came to help me sow peanuts brought his eight-year-old son to drop the red seed into the small holes he was scraping. Children are given miniature hoes to teach them how to produce food from the land.

This seems like a foreign culture now – of sons and daughters helping to grow the family's food. Farming is done on an industrial scale and food can be bought so cheaply that no-one really has any need to raise their own. The idea of children working in the fields might horrify you. But why? It would have been the expected norm prior to the industrial revolution. Children of rural communities in developed countries still skip school when they are needed to bring in the harvest.

The truth is that we are living in a time of plenty. We don't need to grow our own food because it can be bought for a few pounds at the supermarket. Advanced refrigeration and storage techniques mean that I can eat asparagus from Peru, blueberries from Chile and celery from Spain - all in the same meal. Our shopping habits and demand have created this market where food can be flown by jet to our shores and the farmers still make a profit. My local German discount supermarket sells almost every food I'll ever need (not espresso coffee though – don't get me started).

But this current reality has a caveat. And it's a big one: Although we live in stable and plentiful times, there's no guarantee that this will continue indefinitely. In fact, the longer this goes on for, the more likely that we will face real instability. It would only take oil prices to rise due to an unforeseeable conflict or natural disaster and global food prices would skyrocket. And then where would we be?

In Pat Frank's classic, post-apocalyptic thriller *Alas Babylon*, the people of fictional Fort Repose are totally unprepared for nuclear disaster. Even though it was expected (the book is set in the mid 1960's) most are shocked when it happens and then attempt to live their lives normally with disastrous consequences. How much more shocked and unprepared would we be in our post-post-cold war times? If this worries you that's probably a good sign. It means you're awake and alert to worst case scenarios. God forbid we ever see anything like this. But if global instability did take hold, would you know how to feed yourself and your family?

A few generations ago, people in the UK were dying from starvation. There wasn't enough food and it was expensive to buy. Over a million Irish and Scots emigrated to America following the great potato famine which destroyed crops as well as lives. Hunger was a regular feature of life. But now we have the opposite problem: obesity. We have access to too much food. And not just junk food.

Our grandparents and great grandparents would barely be able to believe the abundance of foodstuffs we have access to. My own father, who lived through the second world war, remembers the first time he *saw* a banana. He was 10. Now bananas are a few pennies each.

We live in a time of plenty – don't let anyone tell you otherwise. But will that continue indefinitely? There is a type of cognitive bias called 'continuity bias' which means that we expect the current status quo to remain indefinitely. Whatever has happened will keep happening, right? But that's flawed thinking. The captain of the Titanic was famously quoted as saying he'd never been shipwrecked or *even been close to being shipwrecked*. Tragically, we know what happened to him. People investing in mortgage bonds in the run up to the '07/08 financial crash saw the housing market as a safe bet because it had never nose-dived before. Oh, how wrong they were too.

Nicholas Nassim Taleb's 'Black Swan' event is something that no-one sees coming because they think it's impossible. But how stable is our society and more importantly, our food supply?

Right now, our supply of food is totally dependent on oil. Synthetic fertilisers, farm machinery, delivery vehicles, supermarkets – all need one thing to produce: oil. Which is great. I mean we have total control over all of our oil and none of it comes from unstable places like the Middle East and West Africa, does it?

It wouldn't take much to cut global oil production significantly – think something along the lines of the 1956 Suez Crisis when the Suez Canal was closed to shipping from October 1956 to March 1957. Food prices skyrocket and it becomes a challenge just to put food on the table. Are you ready for that altogether possible scenario? While our recent times have been stable and peaceable, there is no guarantee that this will continue indefinitely. Like a roulette wheel that seems stuck on red, it will switch to black eventually.

**The Tree Stump Philosopher**

"Daddy, what are you doing?" My son sidled over cautiously.

"Digging this stump out." I replied breathlessly. "Want to help?"

The tree – a planted yew - had hard wiry roots and a large, flat root plate. I'd dug a trench about three feet in diameter and was starting to dig and lever up the heavy stump. We'd only moved to the new house a few weeks ago but I wasted no time doing some clearance work on the largely neglected garden. I needed this stump out as I planned to convert the area to a grass lawn for the purposes of football, rugby and tickle fights. But in the meantime, I wanted the land for the first crop of potatoes, beans and turnips.

Before moving I'd longed to live in the country. I'd grown up an urban kid and settled in Glasgow, Scotland's biggest city, when I was in my early twenties. In the limited space and light of the city, growing my own food on any real scale was out of the question.

Back in my new garden I began to think as I dug: How many young men my age or boys my son's age would know how to dig up a stump like this? A few generations ago, most Dads would have been able to clear a plot of ground ready for cultivation. But now I'm in the minority. How do you cultivate (oh dear!) this knowledge. I'm fortunate in that I had a Dad who was a keen gardener. Much of the basics I've learned from him. But if you're less confident when it comes to growing your own food, where do you start? And does any of this even matter?

**Why Living From the Land Matters**

Knowing how to grow and survive from the land is something that is an inherent part of our culture and past. If we lose it it is gone forever. Books and learning can help but are a poor substitute for the way I learned – standing at my father's elbow as he showed me how to dig a plot, plant vegetables and watch them grow into something I wanted to eat.

It doesn't matter if you're heritage is from the Siberian steppes, northern Europe or east Africa, your ancestors depended on the land for their food. Mine were almost certainly farmers back in ancient times, raising animals and crops to feed themselves. My more recent ancestors were farmers too. There is a strong heritable link between you and the land. If you've lost it, isn't it time you got it back?

The best way to teach yourself about growing your own food is to start now and experiment. Gardening books are great but eventually you'll need an iterative approach. That means you learn by doing. These days YouTube provides a wealth of gardening advice - good and bad. There are also a number of excellent books which will give you an insight into how to grow food with minimal outside inputs. I'd recommend you start with *Grow or Die: The Good Guide to Survival Gardening* by David The Good and his prequel *Compost Everything* is also excellent. He does have a US focus but provides plenty for a Northern European like me to think about when it comes to crop selection and garden layout. David the Good's advice is to to master growing high calorie foods (root crops, pumpkins) before graduating to more complex or delicate veggies.

A more international (and considerably more in depth) approach comes from Steve Solomon's *Gardening When it Counts: Growing Food in Hard Times.* Solomon lives on the Australian island of Tasmania but originates from the United States. His focus is more on temperate climates than David The Good's sub-tropical bias. Conventional gardening books and television programmes have some value but often their techniques are too advanced or complicated for the average time-strapped Dad who just wants to learn how to grow things he can eat.

**Return on Investment – Your Wealth is in the Soil**

You've probably heard this asked: 'What's the return on investment on that?'. It's normally used to justify some type of activity. If you value your time, you already care about return on investment even if you've never called it that before. It's a fancy way of saying 'Is this worth my time'? Something with a high ROI (return on investment) has a big benefit from little input.

So what's the ROI on learning how to grow your own food? Here's one way of looking at it: It's a poor return on investment. I can a get a whole sack of potatoes for the same price as washing one of my cars. So why would I spend hours outside growing my own? The supermarket vegetable aisle holds more delicious and genetically perfect produce than I could grow in a lifetime.

What if this misses the point completely? Growing your own food isn't about saving money on your grocery bill. It's about learning (or relearning) a forgotten skill that your ancestors took for granted. As you learn and experiment you use that knowledge to create something (yummy food) *ex nihilo* – out of nothing. Imagine that look in your children's eyes when you show them their first swelling pumpkin or pluck a carrot from the loose sandy soil.

Reconnecting with the land isn't about the destination – in this case having food to eat. It's about the journey; the process you'll go on with your kids; the delight in their eyes and the inevitable disappointment of failed crops. Those are lessons worth learning for now and for the future – whatever it may bring. When the end result is reconnecting with a forgotten past coupled with possible future survival, that return outstrips the time invested a hundred-fold.

A dear friend of mine and agricultural visionary used to say this:

"Your wealth is in the soil."

He meant that everything we need to eat can come from the land and that the soil is a precious life giving super-organism. It's time we reconnected and got our hands dirty.

## How To Use Your Garden to Teach About Life

My favourite part of coming home from boyhood summer holidays was seeing how much my vegetable patch had grown. One year was extra exciting: It was the first year I'd grown radishes. As we pulled into the drive, I bounded out of the car to the back garden. My small allotment was like a jungle and the radish leaves were **ginormous!**

I started pulling to see what size they had grown to. But I was quickly disappointed as I saw that they were all small and deformed little morsels. I'd forgotten to thin out the small plants which meant the crop was a failure. I probably cried – I don't really remember. Being a farmer at any age is tough.

But I learned 2 things. Firstly, always thin out your seedlings or you'll cry. And secondly, sometimes life has bitter disappointment. Things don't always go your way. There aren't always bulbous radishes waiting for you. But you can come back stronger and wiser than before. Don't kid yourself that none of this matter. It does. It matters very much, both now and for the future.

I'm no doomsday prepper, but that doesn't mean I don't believe in being prepared for whatever the future brings. A cursory glance at the history books suggests our time of relative peace is on borrowed time. What comes next? I don't know – but at least I won't go hungry.

## To the Fields!!

Ok, so I stole that line and changed it from the 1990's movie *Robin Hood: Prince of Thieves.* But I do seriously hope that you've been inspired by what you've read in this chapter. You don't need much land to start growing your food. I successfully grew vegetables in my inner-city apartment as a young man. But what you do need is the motivation and perseverance to cope with the 'leafy radishes' that will come your way. Approach as a student and you'll become the master.

**The True Power of the Outdoors Unleashed**

We've covered a lot of ground in this chapter. We started off walking the mountain trails and passes of the Scottish Highlands before going outside to play and finishing by planting our own experimental survival garden.

All of these things were deep and foundational aspects of my childhood which has left me with a sense of their inherent value. This has translated into the way I've started to raise my own children - to value the outdoors - respect and understand its power.

If we have lost the connection with the outdoors, and I firmly believe this to be the case, then isn't it time we reset that balance. The generation we are raising could be the one when these skills disappear altogether into a digital and internet fuelled future where we are increasingly helpless and disconnected with the planet we call home.

**Action:** Make a commitment to join with me - to get your kids outside more, to explore the outdoors and grow something you can eat in the dirt. You'll enrich your life and those around you.

# Pillar 6 - Physical: Fitness, Health and Fat Loss

Why finish this book with a chapter on physical health and fitness? This is a book about strong fatherhood, not being physically strong! Or is it? In this final section, I'll show you why a fit and healthy physical body is fundamental to a father's mission.

Why? Because health and fitness is completely elementary and foundational to nearly every aspect of life. As James Altucher says, in his classic book '*Choose Yourself*', everyone can sleep 8-10 hours, eat less junk food and exercise. But just because everyone can do it, doesn't make it easy. It takes discipline to do all of these things. This is especially the case for us Dads. There are a million reasons why you might not get a good night's sleep, hit the Doritos and skip the gym. I've been there too, but we'll get onto that.

Over the past few years of being a Dad, I've found that when my health is good, everything else works well too - relationships, work, learning and personal development. It all hinges on my physical wellbeing.

In this section, I'm going to cover a range of subjects including the Dad Bod: what it is and what you can do to lose it (or keep it away if you don't have one or don't want it back). I'm also going to go into the benefits of weight training. Weight training is foundational to health and fitness. I'll show you why you should be adding some kind of weight training into your fitness regime.

And a good training programme wouldn't be complete without some good food and I love food. So, I've cooked up some of my favourite recipes including what is probably THE easiest and least messy way to make scrambled eggs. So, let's get started.

## *Chapter 1: The Dad Bod - 'Plus Size' For Men*

The Dad Bod is one of the reasons I started my blog and my overall mission to be a better father. This guy I know was sitting across from me. He leaned back and patted his growing midriff. 'I've got a Dad-Bod now', he said with a degree of triumph. 'It's what you get when you're a Dad'.

In a few short years, we've gone from valuing health, fitness and vitality to relishing poor health and physical disability through intentional weight gain. How did we get here? How did we get to a place where poor health and physical condition is something to be proud of? And what is your response? Before we get to that we need to understand what the Dad Bod is.

### What is the Dad Bod?

I'm going to describe what I see in many men who have a Dad bod. If you think this describes you, maybe it's time for a change. I see it like this: The Dad Bod is mediocrity in father form.

The Dad Bod Dad might go to the gym occasionally or ride his bike to work. But he also eats cake like it's going out of fashion. The closest he comes to 'eating clean' is washing his takeaway tubs before putting them in the recycling. The key thing is he's happy with the situation. The Dad Bod becomes a mindset. For Dad Bod Dad, he has embraced a way of living which is unhealthy. He accepts it because he doesn't know how to change. Or doesn't want to. Instead he exists in a kind of flabby body stasis where he's not obese, not super unhealthy. Just a bit 'meh'. Before you accuse me of being overly judgemental, you should know this: I've been there.

In my early to mid-20's I took almost no care over my physical appearance. I never went to the gym. Apart from a little running now and then and an occasional salad, my diet was primarily fast food, diet sodas and desserts. I was an unhealthy mess. I'd feel lethargic, anxious and would have regular headaches. I drank heavily on the weekends and hated the way I looked - clothed and naked. The problem is that the Dad Bod goes deeper than just physical appearance. It's an image that is bleeding the male energy out of us. Slowly. Silently.

We are meant to be hunters, warriors, protectors and leaders. Your male energy is a limited resource. You can choose to use this energy to be the best man and father you can be. Or you could squander it through unhealthy living and habits.

**The Dad Bod is a Question of Mindset**

The primary problem with the Dad Bod is one of mindset. It's not a question of body-image or whether you look fit or not. It's whether being unhealthy and overweight is a state that you're willing to accept. Those who advocate the Dad Bod say it's OK to have one as nobody really wants to be fit anyway. Plus, life is too busy to be a good Dad *and* be healthy.

You choose one or the other.

What those Dad Bod advocates fail to tell you is this: there is a powerful body of evidence that suggests links between heart disease and various cancers with an unhealthy lifestyle and excess body fat. The World Heart Federation gives this advice:

*"The role of diet is crucial in the development and prevention of cardiovascular disease. Diet is one of the key things you can change that will impact all other cardiovascular risk factors.*

*Comparisons between a diet low in saturated fats, with plenty of fresh fruit and vegetables, and the typical diet of someone living in the developed world show that in the former there is a 73% reduction in the risk of new major cardiac events."*

That's why I strongly advocate a healthy diet. Because basing your eating around healthy carbs, protein and salads will not only help combat the Dad Bod, you're nearly 75% less likely to die from a heart attack.

But it's not just your heart that is affected by poor diet and lifestyle. Weight gain and excess body fat has also been shown to lower testosterone levels and increase levels of oestrogen. Lower testosterone means low energy, reduced sex drive while increased oestrogen means man boobs and water retention. Added to this is an increased risk of type 2 diabetes which comes with its own bingo card of associated health problems. Still thinking a Dad Bod is an intelligent way to live?

**The Dad Bod and The Example for our Children**

When was the last time you saw unfit, unhealthy parents with fit, healthy kids? It's pretty rare, isn't it? A couple of years ago I was in the Netherlands. I saw a whole school of kids and not a single one was overweight. When I saw the parents, it was the same story.

How often do you see significantly overweight kids accompanied by parents who have clearly passed on their bad habits of overeating and inactivity to their offspring? If you pass your good habits on to our children, does the same not happen for the bad ones? If your kids see their Dad constantly chowing down junk foods, full sugar sodas and fried stuff with cheese, they'll think that's acceptable, even normal.

Remember this: there's always an alternative. Don't accept the Dad Bod as inevitable. Instead there are ways that you can defeat the Dad Bod.

**1. You have a choice:**

When I was newly married, someone said to me:

*'Well that's it Neil, you're going to put on lots of weight now you're married'.*

I was stunned. The thought horrified me. I made a decision there and then that I would always strive for health and fitness. As long as I was able, I would keep myself healthy and my weight down. It's a struggle every day. But nothing worth doing is ever easy.

**2. Get a support network:**

If you're the average of your five closest friends, then having friends who share a passion for healthy living and being a good example to their kids is a must. Don't compromise on who you spend time with. Find some other Dads, hang out, eat and be active together. Take your kids.

They'll learn the value of these things quickly.

If you need accountability, find a forum or a likeminded group of guys. There are plenty of men who read my blog ThisDadDoes.com who are committed to improving their health and fitness. Reach out to them and share your ideas and struggles.

**3. Change Your Lifestyle and Your Mindset**

If you don't like something about your lifestyle or your mindset. Change it. Don't wait until the 1st of January or when the time is right. Change what needs to be changed and do it today. You will always be busy, tired, stressed. These are called excuses. Don't be ruled by them.

In the next chapter, I'll explain how I lost my Dad Bod and how you can do the same. If you can't change your lifestyle or mindset, you won't get anywhere. But if you're committed to improving yourself for the benefit of your kids and your own future, you are already strides ahead of those who are happy to accept the Dad bod.

## *Chapter 2: How I Lost My Dad Bod*

Losing my Dad Bod was one of the biggest challenges of my life. It took me hours of discipline, exercise and hard work. The results speak for themselves. Here's my story:

It was January 2013 and I had a Dad Bod. My son had been born six months earlier and it had been stressful. With all the worry and anxiety that comes with a difficult birth and first few weeks of being a Dad, I turned to one comfort I knew well: food. The effects were inevitable. After just six months, I'd gained eight kilograms (about 17.5 lb) of fat without really noticing it.

I'd still been going to the gym, doing cardio and eating enough protein. But I'd also been frequently eating cakes, high calorie protein bars and high carb meals. My training lacked direction and intensity. I had excess body fat and low energy levels. It had been so easy for me to slip into bad habits which now felt impossible to get out of. It would take a drastic turn of events to changing things.

My wakeup call came during a work-based health check. While otherwise healthy, my body fat percentage was pushing into the upper twenties. I remember looking at the nurse in disbelief. How had I managed to put on so much weight in such a short space of time?

### Overhauling Diet was the First Step to Losing the Dad Bod

The first thing I did was change my diet up. I'd been eating a lot of carbohydrate, particularly in the evening. This had consisted of mainly bread and potatoes with some rice and pasta. I had also been eating cakes with wild abandon – my main weakness.

I found a meal plan online and started to follow it. This meant I made the following changes:

- I stopped drinking alcohol
- I stopped eating carbs in the evening

- I controlled portion sizes for protein and carbs
- I cut out most added fats including peanut butter
- I went cold turkey on cakes, desserts and all sweets

I also supplemented with meal replacement shakes which helped fill me up between whole food meals. Along with this I took a fat burner, fish oils and a green tea/CLA formula.

My meal plan looked like this:

**Breakfast**: Eggs and oatmeal or toast

**Mid Morning**: Meal replacement shake

**Lunch**: Chicken, wholewheat pasta, broccoli

**Mid Afternoon**: Meal replacement shake

**Evening Meal**: Ground beef with tomatoes and onions, mixed veg

**Before bed**: Low fat Greek Yogurt

The result? I started to lose fat quickly. At the beginning of the programme I was losing 2lbs a week. As my body adjusted from eating all that junk I was tired and hungry and had serious cravings. But after a few weeks I found I was less hungry between meals and could focus more on my daily activities.

As a general rule of thumb, losing weight will make you hungry throughout the day. That is a rough (but fairly accurate) way to gauge if you're getting your calorie intake right. If you're getting peckish in the run up to your next meal, your body is having to work hard to find its energy and that deficit will make you burn more fat.

I pre-prepared all my meals when I was out traveling or at work. I cut out things like protein bars, many of which are vegetable fats with a little bit of protein and add a lot of calories. I also drank three to five litres of water a day. As I was eating relatively low carbohydrate meals, I would have a re-feed every two weeks. I would loosen up my diet and eat more carbs. This wasn't a cheat but a way to make sure my body was getting the nutrients I needed.

### Being Disciplined in my Exercise Programme Helped me Shift my Dad Bod

I didn't just want to lose weight. I wanted to get lean and fit at the same time. In the years before becoming a Dad I'd trained in Muay Thai, trail running and the gym. I wanted the leanness of being a fighter back. And I wanted to keep as much muscle as possible.

I trained six times a week split between cardio and light weights or circuits. For cardio, I would either go running or do a bodyweight circuit. My runs consisted of either Fartlek (interval) training or hill sprints. In the weights room, I did an upper body day and a lower body day. One feature of this 12-week period is that I didn't miss a single training session. I would go running, even in horizontal sleet, rain, wind (remember, I started in January). If I had a busy day ahead, I would get up early and train before my wife and son were awake. If I travelled, I took either running or gym clothes. I was motivated to succeed and this motivation manifested itself in a discipline where failure became unthinkable to me. I would visualise how I wanted to look and feel which was especially important on the days I didn't want to train or was busy.

At the end of the twelve weeks, I was down to eighteen percent body fat but had maintained most of my muscle mass. I'd lost an incredible eight kilograms (around 18lbs!) and felt amazing. I showed my 'after' photo to a friend who refused to believe it was real. He couldn't believe how good I looked. When I tried to use the pictures in a Facebook advert for my blog, they were banned for being 'unrealistic'.

### Finding Balance and Overdoing Things

My Dad Bod fat loss wasn't all plain sailing. A few weeks into my diet and exercise programme, it was clear I was overdoing it. I was losing weight very rapidly (2.5 kilograms in one week) and feeling extremely lethargic. So, I started to increase the amount of fat in the form of peanut butter and a little regular butter on the days I ate whole-wheat toast. My weight loss slowed to a more sensible level and energy levels got back to normal.

It was an important lesson for me to remember to listen to my body. Sudden, rapid weight loss and very low energy levels can be a warning sign that you are over training. If this happens to you, stop and think what you need to do to fix it. Adding in a few extra calories or getting to bed earlier may be the best solution. Don't overdo it and don't over train. Otherwise you risk illness and burnout.

### Final Thoughts on Fast Dad Bod Loss

Hopefully this story can inspire you to make a change. 12 weeks is a short period of time to lose the amount of fat that I did and that's not the way for everyone. In fact, I'd recommend losing weight over a much longer period of time. It's more sustainable to build small changes into your lifestyle than go on rapid weight loss that can make your rebound and gain all the weight back.

Remember:

1. Commit to making a change in your lifestyle - don't wait for the first of January. Now is as good a time as any.
2. Be disciplined in your eating and exercise. Wanting to give up is normal. Whether you succeed or not depends on your ability to persevere.
3. Don't overdo things. Better to make small, sustainable changes to your lifestyle than go on fad diets and regret it later.

## *Chapter 3: Losing the Dad Bod 2.0 - In it for the Long Run*

Nearly four years after the events I described in chapter 2, it's only right that I look at the follow up. Once you've managed to lose the weight that you wanted and live the life you've wanted to live, how do you keep going?

An ancient proverb goes like this:

*"It's easier to stay on top of the mountain than to climb there in the first place."*

Hopefully if you're reading this book, you are already committed to living a healthy lifestyle for yourself and the benefit of your kids and loved ones as part of your father's mission. That's a big driver for me - to be healthy and active so that I can give my children the childhood they deserve.

So, it saddens me when I see overweight or inactive parents. I can make a safe assumption that their kids are going to miss out on the kind of active, adventurous childhood that I took for granted. That's why physical fitness is so important - because it affects everything else you do. That's why it comes first in this book. Health and fitness is foundational if you want to fulfil your father's mission.

So how do you make sure that you're staying fit and healthy for the long run? Hopefully you're only going to have to lose your Dad Bod once. The rest of your life will be making small and continuous adjustments to your lifestyle to stop it coming back.

### Living the Dad Bod Free Lifestyle: Systems over Goals

A Dad Bod free lifestyle comes down to one main idea. Commitment. If you are committed to live a life which is aimed at promoting longevity, energy and overall health are you more or less likely to have a Dad Bod? Whether your Dad Bod comes back or not depends on the systems you put in place. But too many men focus on goals instead of systems when it comes to living healthily.

Writer and businessman Scott Adams doesn't think much of goals:

*"To put it bluntly, goals are for losers. That's literally true most of the time. If your goal is to lose ten pounds, you will spend every moment until you reach the goal – if you reach it at all – feeling as if you were short of your goal."*

Scott Adams - *How to Fail at Almost Everything and Still Win Big* (2013).

Instead, Adams suggests putting systems in place to allow you to achieve whatever you want to achieve. Thankfully this example already uses the topic we are on - weight loss. For Adams, the preferred approach is 'systems based'. This means making small adjustments to your lifestyle to help you make gradual and continued progress. This might mean getting rid of all junk food in the house and only buying it for special occasions or treats. Or it could mean joining a gym which is on the way to (or from) your work. After all, are you more likely to go to the gym if you pass the door twice a day?

For the long term, a system based approach works much better than setting goals. That's because these systems become habits. Your gym attendance, healthy eating and regular sleep patterns become habits. Whereas you get out of the habit of drinking heavily, eating junk in the evenings or finishing the kid's dinners when they're in bed.

What is the advantage of something positive forming a habit? If you do something positive out of habit, you do it almost without thinking. Here's an example. Hopefully you clean your teeth on a regular basis. And I'll bet you do it at the same time, same place every single day. That's a habit. And an important one at that. If it wasn't a habit, you'd forget all the time. And then you'd wake up wondering why you had stinky breath and all your teeth were falling out. Keeping the Dad Bod away is no different. Your positive lifestyle changes become habits. You don't even think about eating healthy foods, lifting weights and doing cardio. It's just what you do.

**Small Changes are Better than Big Ones**

Wait, is that right? Small changes are better than big changes? Yes, if the small changes are sustainable. If you can make several small changes over a long period of time, this will have a greater influence over your lifestyle than one big change that can't last. That's why extreme fad diets don't work. Their effects are so drastic that they can't be sustained. And so the weight piles back on.

I know a few people who lost a huge amount of weight. And they did it by making small changes. One friend started eating salads at lunch instead of sandwiches and running 10 minutes on the treadmill at home. He looks great and hasn't gained his weight back in five years. Meanwhile everyone I know who does the faddy diet circuit rebounds more than an NBA star. And they look worse.

**Summary - Have a System for Dad Bod Loss 2.0**

How do you develop a system? Because I can't know your individual situation, I can't give you specifics. But I can tell you aspects of my system that have helped me stay Dad Bod free for a while now.

These are:

- Eat regular, home cooked meals (4 per day works for me)
- Train for no more than an hour a day, 5 days a week
- Drink plenty of water, coffee and sugar free soda
- Limit sweets and treats to the weekend
- Give complex carbs a miss after 4 pm
- Train at the same times of day
- Do exercise that I enjoy
- Enjoy life

There's more to it than just this but I wanted to give you a taste of how I organise myself. If it looks like a lot of work, it is. But I didn't develop this overnight. It's only by making small gradual changes that fit with my lifestyle and timetable that I've been able to see real and lasting results.

## *Chapter 4: Why You Should Probably be Lifting Weights*

Hopefully by now you have a fair idea that weight training is a good idea. It will not only make you stronger, leaner and more muscular, it has a whole range of other health benefits that I'm going to cover in this chapter.

Weight training doesn't need to mean long weight sessions in a grimy, bodybuilder's gym either. Adding some form of resistance (even your own bodyweight) will have a dramatic impact on your physique and health. If you want to know more, keep reading.

### Confession Time

I'll admit it, I haven't always lifted weights. In fact, I wasn't even a regular at a gym until a few years ago. Here's my story of how I started lifting weights.

I'd just started a new job - a pastoral worker in a church. One of my projects was to set up and run a small gym in the basement of the church building. The only problem was I hadn't set foot in a gym since I was 14 years old! This had to change, and fast. So, I enrolled at the local university gym and, armed with a basic programme, started lifting light dumbbells and using the resistance machines. Looking back, my workouts sucked. I didn't know what I was doing but I still make the inevitable 'newbie gains' that you can expect if you've never weight trained before.

With that bit of knowledge, I started working out harder and harder. I moved to training full time in the basement gym. It took adaptability and ingenuity to have a good workout but those skills stood me in good stead for the future - having to figure out a way to train your body with limited resources is an underrated skill.

I eventually moved back to training in a University gym where I began to increase the consistency and focus of my workouts. I used Jim

Wendler's 5/3/1 strength training programme and I still use it today. My body and mind has changed dramatically from that first day in the gym.

The point of this story is this: I got to weight training **late.** I was well into my mid-twenties before I picked up anything heavier than a petrol can. But in those six years, I've seen changes in my body that I was not prepared for. And it seems to get better as I get older. I'm now realising the physique and build I wanted and have learned how to get there in the most efficient way possible. But how does this happen? And how can you get your own slice of the action?

### 1. Lift Weights for Increased Metabolism

When you lift weights, you will gain muscle. This is true especially when you're new to weight training. I experienced this at first and it was a thrill. Your body will be super responsive to the new stimulus and you'll pack on muscle in double quick time.

Sadly, this honeymoon period only lasts for a few months. But if you stick with the training and keep your diet under control, you could add 10-15 pounds of muscle in your first year of training.
But what does this have to do with metabolism? According to Wikipedia, Metabolism is:

*"All chemical reactions that occur in living organisms, including digestion and the transport of substances into and between different cells."*

Different types of body tissue have different levels of activity when it comes to metabolism. Muscle has lots of chemical reactions just to keep going whereas stored bodyfat is fairly inert. It just sits there doing not very much, not burning energy like muscle can.

So, if you weigh 75 kilos and are 25% body fat your body is going to burn a lot less energy throughout the day than if you were the same weight but 15% body fat. Your metabolism would have increased because of the extra muscle you're packing. With an increased metabolism comes the ability to eat more food without getting fat and an improved fat burning process. So, it's one big win for metabolism.

### 2. Lift Weights to Become Stronger

When I posted this quote on my blog, it caused a lot of laughs:

*"I don't really like being stronger. I'm much happier being weak...."* – No One. Ever.

After all, who doesn't want to get stronger? If you're a Dad, increased strength is going to help you out a lot for things like:

- Pushing your teenage daughter's car when it breaks down
- Carrying all of the holiday luggage. In one trip
- Opening stubborn jars of jam
- General awesomeness

Strength can be a by-product of lifting weights, particularly when you start out. Your strength will skyrocket to begin with. However, it will start to tail off eventually and you'll 'plateau'. This is when you aren't really making any improvements in strength. You then may have to train specifically to get stronger. Like metabolism, increased strength has a positive benefit on your health including increased bone density and improved mental health.

### 3. Lift Weights to Be More than You Are

Life is full of choices. When it comes to weight training you can:

1. Not lift weights and remain the skinny and weak person that can lift weights but doesn't because you're too lazy, unmotivated or pathetic. In one year, you'll be exactly who you are today, but one year older.

2. Start lifting weights and become disciplined. In the process, you lower your body fat, increase muscle size, sex drive and overall attractiveness. In one year, you'll be older, but you'll look and feel younger.

Self-Improvement books sell like hot cakes. Titles like '*The Chimp Paradox*' sold thousands of copies and topped the best seller's lists in 2015 and 2016. But one of the easiest ways to improve yourself is to train your body into a fitter, healthier, better version of what you are now. It's not easy – that's why everyone would rather just buy a book and read it on the train while they eat half a packet of chocolate biscuits for breakfast. You can choose not to be that Dad. You can choose to refuse the Dad Bod and instead commit to real, lasting, physical self-help.

**4. Lift Weights for More Motivation**

Wait? Lifting weights increases motivation? Yes, but not necessarily how you might think. Lifting weights will give you a greater sense of purpose and discipline (see point 3). But what I'm talking about now is increased testosterone.

Testosterone (or 'test' for short) is the male sex hormone. And guess what? If you're lifting weights and eating the right foods, your body secretes more of it. More testosterone means more muscle, increased sex drive and lower body fat. Higher testosterone also means smaller man boobs. And you can't put a price on that. Will more test make you aggressive? In a word, no.

You would need to be enhancing testosterone chemically for that to be an issue. I'm talking about small increases in hormone levels due to lifestyle and diet changes. The benefits of a hormonally balanced lifestyle are like the pot of gold at the end of the rainbow, the light at the end of the tunnel. Once you've experienced this you'll never go back. You'll be more motivated because you **always** want to feel this way.

### 5. Lift Weights for Better Health

I used to think that I would lift weights for a few years and then quit and take up jogging or cycling instead. I, like many people, thought that lifting weights would ultimately lead to crippling injury and early death.

But the more I learn, the more I know this to be false. The only people who have crippling injury are the really unlucky or really stupid lifters. Everyone else can carry on indefinitely.
I recently went to a funeral. This guy had lifted weights beyond his ninetieth birthday! It was a part of his lifestyle, something he always did. Like brushing his teeth or taking a shower.

I'd be an idiot to think I'll always lift heavy and train for increasing strength. But I do intend on lifting as long as physically able. The benefits easily outweigh any risks. A phrase I've used before is the J.O.D. - The Jacked Old Dude. You'll see them from time to time. They are older men who have an impressively lean and muscular physique. They look good because they've learned how to train **and** look after their bodies. That's the knowledge I crave and I'll willingly spend the next 10 years trying to get it.

### Closing Thoughts - Confessions of a Reluctant Lifter

Imagine a reluctant gym user. That was me. I was probably one of the most reluctant gym go-ers at the start of my lifting career. But the changes to my body and life in general have proved too much to ignore.

In the gym, you become able to shut out problems and focus on the task at hand. You will always leave feeling calmer and glad you trained. The feeling of being strong, powerful and 'together' cannot be valued. Hopefully I've convinced you that you should take up weight training. If you do, let me know how you get on.

References:


1. https://www.ncbi.nlm.nih.gov/pubmed/16702776
2. https://www.ncbi.nlm.nih.gov/pubmed/6319947

## *Chapter 5 – Recipes for Hard Working Dads*

I enjoy cooking and preparing food. But I also have strict criteria for what I'm prepared to fix. The food that I prepare must be:

**Simple**: If it's too complicated or has more than six or seven ingredients, I'm not really interested. Life is too short for me to spend time fixing an elaborate gourmet dinner. If you get a kick out of that, then great. It's not my bag.

**Healthy**: This should go without saying. I like a treat/cheat meal every so often but healthy food just makes my body sing. Whole foods and vegetables in particular will have such a drastic effect on your metabolism and digestion that you'll wonder why you ever gave them a body swerve.

**Fast**: I'm not talking about a drive thru burger joint. When I make food, it needs to take me the minimum amount of time. As a hardworking Dad, time is always at a premium. I haven't got hours to spend making something to eat. I go into the kitchen, do my thing, then get out.

This isn't going to turn into a book of recipes. Instead I'm going to go through a simple recipe for breakfast, lunch and dinner. Hopefully you'll be inspired to seek out more simple recipes and try them for yourself. There are all these recipes and more on my website www.thisdaddoes.com.

### Breakfast: Easy Microwave Scrambled Eggs

I love scrambled eggs. If I was limited to one food forever, scrambled eggs would be up there. What I don't like is mess: scrubbing the pan for ages with little bits of burnt egg all encrusted onto the bottom. There has to be a better way. And there is. Now I make scrambled eggs exclusively in the microwave. Here's how:

### Scrambled Eggs – A High Protein Hit

If you're working and training hard you'll need extra protein. Supplements are fine, but your main source of protein should be from whole foods. Eggs are a great choice because:

- They're cheap – buy in bulk and they're a few pence each.
- They have top protein. Egg protein is used as the benchmark for protein quality.
- They also contain saturated and unsaturated fats as well as vitamin D – all of which are necessary for male sex hormone production.

One large egg = around 7 grams of protein. Have 3, scrambled with cheese on a whole-wheat bagel and you have a breakfast of champions. The only problem is making them. As I've noted already, scrambling in a pan is messy. Get the microwave settings wrong and you're looking at a grey, rubbery mess. You might as well have stuck with the 'Special K'.

**How to Microwave Scrambled Eggs**

This recipe is the product of years of trial and error. I've got it cracked (oh dear) now to the point where I get it right every time. Keep reading to find out how you too can become a Whisking Wizard (too much?).

To make my microwave scrambled eggs, you will need:

- 3 Large Eggs
- 30ml Milk
- 1 tbsp Butter or Coconut Oil
- 1 Slice of Low fat Cheese

1. Grease a microwaveable bowl with the butter or oil. This should be large enough to accommodate the cooked eggs – they will expand!
2. Add the eggs and milk and mix together to break up the egg yolks.
3. Microwave on full power for 90 seconds. Take out and stir to break up any cooked bits of egg.

4. Microwave again on full power for 40 seconds then take out and stir. Repeat this until the eggs are cooked and light an fluffy (probably another 2 or three 40-second blasts).
5. Break up cheese and stir into the hot eggs. Spread on a high protein bagel or an English muffin. Enjoy.

Outrageously simple, isn't it? You can now make scrambled eggs even if you've sucked at it before. I've shared this recipe on my blog and YouTube channel and the feedback has been great - it works every time and can even be a nice treat. Add in a couple of slices of high protein or sprouted bread and you've got a winning combination.

You could do this the night before work for a snack or even make it for your kids if you're in a rush (mine love scrambled eggs). Why not experiment with other cheeses or adding spices such as cumin or chilli for a bit of extra flavour?

**Lunch: Easy Mexican Chicken and Rice**

If you care about what you eat for lunch then it makes sense to prep your meals in advance. Doing this in bulk saves effort, time and money. This is one of my go-to bulk cooking recipes for healthy, high protein lunches.

You will need:

- Diced chicken breast – 180-200g raw weight per meal.
- White rice (I like American long grain - tastes like freedom) 50g per meal
- 1/2 packet of Mexican fajita spice mix
- 1-2 tablespoons olive oil
- A large bowl
- Baking tray lined with foil

Now you have all the ingredients, it's time to start making the meals. For bulk prepping, I like to put on classical music as I cook. If it's evening I might even have a glass of wine and read a good book while I'm waiting.

1. Mix the chicken, oil and spice packet in the bowl making sure all the chicken is coated in the spice mix.

2. Preheat your oven to 200 C (430 F).

3. Spread the chicken evenly across the baking tray.

4. Place in the oven for 20 minutes until cooked.

5. Weigh out the rice and place in a pan of water (use a rice cooker if you have one). Use double the volume of water to rice.

6. Boil the rice until the water has evaporated (around 20 minutes). Add more water if required for a longer cook.

7. Remove the chicken and rice from the heat and divide equally into tubs. Allow to cool before putting in the fridge or freezer.

Simple, isn't it? You can eat hot or cold although I'd recommend heating rice thoroughly before eating as it could make you very ill otherwise. If you don't like rice you could use quinoa or whole wheat pasta or noodles. What's missing from this? Green stuff, right? OK, you got me. It's not that I don't like veggies, I just don't like eating them in my prepped meals. Sitting in my car eating cold chicken and rice is bad enough without adding rubbery broccoli.

I make up for it through drinking green shakes in the morning and eating vegetables and salad for the last meal of the day. If you think this is degenerate behaviour, feel free to send me an angry email.

**Dinner: Really Easy Liver and Bacon**

This recipe for liver and bacon is one of my favourites. It's quick and easy. It's also clean, protein packed and cheap (serves 2 and 2 kids).

Ingredients

- 400g Lamb's liver
- 2 rashers of back or turkey bacon, chopped
- 1 large white onion, sliced
- 1/2 a medium white or savoy cabbage, chopped
- 100ml Low sodium vegetable stock
- 2 tbsp red wine vinegar
- 1 tsp English mustard
- 3 tbsp olive or rapeseed oil

Step 1. Add 1tbsp of olive to a frying pan and fry the onions and bacon over a medium heat until the bacon is cooked and the onions are soft. Set aside.

Step 2. Remove the liver from its packaging and use kitchen roll to soak up any excess liquid. Add 1tbsp oil to pan and sear liver in batches on a high heat.

Step 3. Turn the heat down and add to the liver the onions, bacon, stock, vinegar and mustard. Simmer lightly until the sauce is reduced and thickened.

Step 4. While this is happening add remaining oil to a large wok and add cabbage. Sauté until the cabbage has softened. Add a little water and cover. Once cabbage is cooked, serve on a plate with the liver and bacon mix on top.

You could also try serving with kale instead of cabbage. I like to cook my kale in a similar way with a little chopped red onion. If you end up with leftovers, why not try it for breakfast with scrambled eggs to give you energy for those morning workouts.

**A Father's Mission is a Healthy One**

It's hard to describe how important health and fitness is to your life as a father and as a man. If you are low energy and feel overweight and generally crap all the time, are you going to be at your best when it comes to life?

You have a mission to fulfil and being an unhealthy slob isn't going to help you. I can't make any decisions for you but what I will say is this: since I took my health seriously, my quality of life has improved significantly.

And if you struggle with the discipline to exercise and eat right, guess what? So do I. But that doesn't mean you quit. It means you find ways to make it easier for you to live a healthy lifestyle, for your and for your children's sake.

## Now Go and Fulfil Your Father's Mission

By now you should have figured out how you're going to implement the changes you need to make in your life to become the best Dad you can be. When I wrote the first draft of this book, I didn't include the actions at the end of the chapters.

But as I came back to edit the book (yes, I did that all myself) I realised that I'd missed a fundamental part of the process out. If you read this book but have no intention of putting any of what you've learned into practice, it's been a wasted journey.

By now you should have realised you have a mission as a father that you need to fulfil. No book can improve your lifestyle or your vision for your life. Only you can choose to do that for yourself and for those you love. Whether that means living a more spiritual life, taking care of your mental or physical health or maybe just facing a fear or two every now and then, this next part is up to you.

I firmly believe that almost every one of us is born with the ability to be an adequate and loving father. The fact that you've read this book shows that you care about being more than adequate. And in that thought is my raison d'etre - that there are Dads who are quite happy bumping along the bottom of 'adequate'.

You'll meet these types of Dads all the time. Maybe you were one before reading this short book. But there is a flipside to that type of flaccid fatherhood: There are Dads who want to put a polish on fatherhood so that they can be the best. They are the few, the elite.

Writing this book has been my pleasure and I hope that in reading it, you have found enjoyment and challenge in equal measure. But don't make this the end of your journey. Make it the beginning as you embark on a new era of committed, strong fatherhood in our modern times.

We need more Dads like this: Dads who are committed to personal improvement. Dads who are relentless in discipline and in raising their kids right. Dads who take care of themselves for the benefit of those they love. That's you and me: Dads who do more.

19387227R00088

Printed in Great Britain
by Amazon